LIVING ROOMS

Living rooms
Trends & tradition

PIET SWIMBERGHE

PHOTOGRAPHY BY

JAN VERLINDE

LANNOO

CONTENTS

LIVING ROOM

IEMAND VERTELDE ME ooit dat zijn woning een groot kamerscherm is, waarachter hij zich verbergt voor de buitenwereld. Hij ontvangt graag vrienden, maar wanneer hij thuiskomt, hoeft hij de buitenwereld even niet en wil hij wegdromen in zijn eigen wereld. Deze woning staat trouwens in dit boek. Hoewel de woonruimte aan een straat grenst, zijn er geen vensters aan de straatkant, enkel aan de tuinzijde. De woning lijkt op een moderne versie van de prehistorische *rock shelter*: intiem en beschermend. Dit 'antieke' menselijke gevoel is een essentieel onderdeel van de ideale woonruimte. Daarom is de living room misschien nog intiemer dan de slaapruimte. Vele slaapkamers zijn arm aangekleed, met weinig meer dan een bed, een stoel en een kast. De living room is boeiender en weerspiegelt het karakter van zijn bewoners. Ik laat het aan de lezers over om uit te vissen wie ontspannen chaotisch is of een afgemeten en streng leven leidt.

In dit boek brengen fotograaf Jan Verlinde en ikzelf wat we 'een verzameling fascinerende woonruimtes met een persoonlijk karakter' noemen samen. De stijl speelt niet zo'n rol, ze zijn allemaal ongeveer hedendaags, klassiek of modern, maar vooral mooi en hebben uitstraling: het zijn geen showrooms.

We merken dat de living room de laatste jaren van gedaante verandert. De woonruimte wordt ruimer dan de zithoek alleen. Je hebt weinig aparte eetkamers, maar leefkeukens waarin je vrienden ontvangt. We werken meer thuis, op verschillende plekken, met de laptop op de keukentafel of aan een geïmproviseerd bureau. Deze evolutie is al een tijdje aan de gang, waardoor de living space zich straks over de hele woning uitbreidt. We keren terug naar eeuwen geleden, toen grote huizen slechts één grote leefruimte hadden waarin alles gebeurde, van rusten tot koken. In de achttiende en negentiende eeuw werden die functies meer en meer gescheiden.

De wijze waarop we eten weerspiegelt de wijze waarop we wonen. Tot voor enkele jaren was de fusion kitchen, die verschillende eetculturen samenbrengt, nog niet aan de orde en zwoeren gourmands bij de 'service à la russe', met een strikte opeenvolging van gerechten, van voorgerecht tot nagerecht. Dit systeem werd rond 1810 populair in Parijs en verving de 'service à la française', waarbij alle gerechten ineens op tafel verschenen. Met andere woorden: alles werd netjes van elkaar afgescheiden, voorgerecht van de hoofdschotels. Nu is ook de zitruimte niet langer de enige leefruimte en leven we op vele plaatsen tegelijk. Soms door plaatsgebrek, want wie een krap bemeten flat in Parijs betrekt, moet goochelen met ruimte. Het gaat erom dat we relaxt omspringen met de functies en het overal gezellig en spannend maken. Laat dit boek een heerlijke inspiratiebron zijn voor uw interieur!

Un jour, quelqu'un m'a confié que pour lui, sa maison était comme un grand paravent derrière lequel il se dérobait au monde extérieur. Tout en recevant volontiers des amis, il préfère néanmoins abandonner le monde extérieur devant sa porte et réserver l'espace intérieur pour s'adonner à ses propres rêves. Cette maison figure d'ailleurs dans ce livre. Bien que l'espace de vie jouxte la rue, il n'y a pas de fenêtres côté rue mais uniquement côté jardin. Cette demeure ressemble à une version moderne de l'abri rocheux préhistorique fournissant protection et intimité. C'est pourquoi le séjour est peut-être encore plus intime que la chambre à coucher. De nombreuses chambres à coucher ont une décoration modeste avec souvent guère plus qu'un lit, une chaise et une armoire. Le séjour est bien plus passionnant par la façon dont il reflète le caractère de ses habitants. On laissera le soin aux lecteurs de découvrir lequel de nos personnages mène une existence décontractée et chaotique ou plutôt une vie bien ordonnée et mesurée.

Dans ce livre, le photographe Jan Verlinde et moi-même avons réuni ce que nous appelons une collection d'habitations fascinantes par leur caractère personnel. Plutôt que par le style assez uniformément contemporain, classique ou moderne, elles se font remarquer par la personnalité qu'elles dégagent : ce ne sont pas du tout des showrooms.

Il semble bien que la salle de séjour ait changé d'apparence au cours de ces dernières années. L'espace de vie ne se limite plus au seul salon. Les salles à manger séparées se font rares, par contre les cuisines s'ouvrent jusqu'à y accueillir les repas entre amis. On travaille aussi davantage à la maison, l'ordinateur portable posé sur la table de cuisine ou sur un bureau improvisé. Cette évolution est en cours depuis un certain temps et on pourrait dire qu'en élargissant l'espace vital à la maison entière, on vit un retour vers un lointain passé où les grandes demeures avaient un vaste espace de vie qui accueillaient toutes les activités, de la préparation des repas jusqu'au repos. C'est à partir des dix-huitième et dix-neuvième siècles que ces fonctions se sont progressivement séparées.

Le style des repas reflète la façon dont nous habitons. Jusqu'à il y a quelques années, il n'était pas encore question de 'fusion cuisine' qui réunit différentes cultures culinaires et les fins gourmets tenaient au 'service à la russe' avec, du hors d'œuvre au dessert, un stricte succession des mets. Remplaçant le 'service à la française' où tous les mets apparaissaient en même temps à table, cette façon de faire était devenue très populaire à Paris vers 1810. Depuis lors, tout était donc bien séparé, hors d'œuvre et plats principaux. Actuellement, le salon/séjour n'est plus le seul espace de vie et nous vivons à plusieurs endroits en même temps. Parfois par manque de place comme lorsqu'il faut jongler avec les espaces dans un appartement parisien aux dimensions modestes. Mais il s'agit d'aborder sans crispation les différentes fonctions du lieu et de créer partout une ambiance conviviale et passionnante. Que ce livre puisse servir de merveilleuse source d'inspiration pour l'aménagement intérieur dont rêve sans doute chaque lecteur !

Someone once told me that his home was a large folding screen, behind which he hid from the outside world. He liked receiving friends, but on coming home he had no need of the outside world and wanted to dream off into his own one. His home is also in this book. Although the living room lies on a street, there are no street-facing windows, only on the garden side. His home is, as it were, a modern version of the prehistoric rock shelter: intimate and protective. This 'ancient' human feeling is an essential part of the ideal living room. For this reason the living room of a home is perhaps even more intimate than a bedroom. Many bedrooms are sparsely decorated, with little more than a bed, a chair and a wardrobe. The living room is more exciting and reflects the character of its inhabitants. I will leave it to readers to figure out which of the people whose living rooms are featured in this book lead relaxed and chaotic lives and which live structured and rigorous ones.

In this book, photographer Jan Verlinde and I put together what we call a collection of fascinating living rooms with a personal touch. It is not the particular style that is so important, they are all pretty much contemporary, classic or modern, but they are beautiful and have character: they are not showrooms.

We note that the living room has changed shape in recent years. The living area is becoming larger than the sitting room proper. We have few separate dining rooms, but rather kitchens in which we receive friends. We work more at home, in different parts of the house, with the laptop on the kitchen table or at a makeshift desk. This trend has been with us for some time, with the living room steadily expanding throughout the house. We are reverting to the situation of centuries ago when large houses had only a single large living area in which everything took place, from sleeping to cooking. In the eighteenth and nineteenth centuries, these functions were increasingly separated.

The way we eat reflects the way we live. Until a few years ago, mixing cuisines and culinary cultures was not yet accepted, and gourmets still swore by the 'service à la russe', with a strict succession of dishes from hors d'oeuvre through to dessert, that became popular in Paris around 1810, replacing the 'service à la française' where all the dishes appeared at once on the table. In other words, everything was neatly separated, hors d'oeuvre from the main dishes. Today the living area is not just the living or sitting room and we live in many places simultaneously. Sometimes simply because of lack of room, because if you live in a cramped Paris flat you have to juggle with space. The main thing is to have a relaxed attitude to these different domestic functions and make living fun and exciting. Let this book be a wonderful source of inspiration for your own interior!

FORNASETTI

FORNASETTI'S OASE

Deze oase uit de jaren vijftig is weer helemaal van deze tijd, nu heel wat interieurontwerpers het saaie minimalisme loslaten en barokke stijlen herontdekken. Hier stappen we door de metafysische woning van de Milanese ontwerper Piero Fornasetti. We zijn te gast bij zijn zoon Barnaba, die het pand niet alleen bewoont, maar het ook dagelijks als atelier gebruikt en er eveneens het oeuvre van zijn beroemde vader wereldwijd doet herleven. De wervelende ontwerpen van Piero, met zuilen, letters, neoklassieke ornamenten en portretten, zijn weer in en inspireren ook nieuwe ontwerpers. De woning ligt in een rustige buurt achter een flatgebouw in Milaan, en telt heel wat zit- en werkhoeken die door Piero afhankelijk van de warmte, het licht en het uur van de dag werden gebruikt. Hij zat nooit stil en voegde overal wat aan toe. Alles werd versierd door zijn hand. De meeste decoraties bracht hij zelf aan. Hij verzamelde ook allerlei objecten. De talrijke deuren, gangen en spiegels zorgen voor extra diepte. Het interieur is metafysisch, bijna surreëel en ook gewoon gezellig voor wie van drukte houdt. Vooral het gele constructivistische bureau is schitterend. Het is Bauhausachtig, maar heerlijk rijk opgedirkt. Ook de zithoek, op één hoog, met de bibliotheek en het prachtige kamerscherm, is een mysterieuze plek. De woning is groot, maar smal en opgebouwd uit een enfilade van vertrekken die je telkens in een andere sfeer brengen. Op deze inspirerende verscheidenheid kunnen we alleen maar jaloers zijn: dit is puur visueel genot. Wie smetvrees heeft en bang is voor wat versiering ontgaat de schoonheid van deze plek.

L'OASIS DE FORNASETTI

Cette oasis des années cinquante est de nouveau tout à fait branchée depuis que beaucoup de décorateurs d'intérieur abandonnent le minimalisme ennuyeux et redécouvrent des styles baroques. On traverse ici la demeure métaphysique du styliste milanais Piero Fornasetti où nous accueille son fils Barnaba qui ne se contente pas de l'habiter puisqu'il l'utilise à son tour quotidiennement comme atelier et quartier général pour faire revivre dans le monde entier l'œuvre de son célèbre père. Avec ses colonnes, ses lettres, les ornements et portraits néoclassiques, les créations virevoltantes de Piero ont reconquis le devant de la scène et inspirent aussi de nouveaux créateurs. Située dans un quartier calme derrière un immeuble à Milan, la maison compte de nombreux espaces de travail et de vie que Piero utilisait tous en fonction de la chaleur, de la lumière et de l'heure du jour. Ne se tenant jamais tranquille, il ne cessait d'ajouter partout des éléments. Il décorait tout, la plupart du temps lui-même. Et il collectionnait aussi des objets très divers. Par ailleurs, le grand nombre de portes, de couloirs et de miroirs confèrent beaucoup de profondeur aux espaces. L'intérieur est métaphysique, presque surréel et aussi tout simplement convivial si on aime l'agitation. On retient cependant surtout le superbe bureau constructiviste jaune, du genre Bauhaus mais avec une décoration merveilleusement riche. Au premier, le coin salon avec la bibliothèque et le superbe paravent est aussi un endroit mystérieux. Grande mais étroite, la maison est constituée d'une enfilade de pièces qui créent chacune une ambiance différente. Cette diversité inspiratrice ne peut que nous rendre jaloux : c'est du pur plaisir visuel. Mais la beauté de ce lieu échappe probablement à celui qui craint le microbe de la décoration.

FORNASETTI'S OASIS

This fifties oasis is again contemporary, now that many interior decorators are abandoning boring minimalism and rediscovering baroque styles. Here we step through the metaphysical home of Milanese designer Piero Fornasetti. We are the guests of his son Barnaba, who not only lives in the building, using it daily as a workshop, but is also reviving the work of his famous father for consumption worldwide. Piero's swirling designs, with their columns, letters, neoclassical ornaments and portraits, are again in and also inspiring new designers. The home is located in a quiet area behind an apartment building in Milan, with many different sitting and working corners that were used by Piero according to the temperature, light and time of day. He never sat still and was always adding new touches everywhere. Everything was decorated by his hand. He also collected all kinds of objects. The many doors, corridors and mirrors provide extra depth. The interior is metaphysical, almost surreal and simply nice for those who like to feel crowded. The yellow constructivist office in particular is magnificent, Bauhaus-like, but richly dressed. The first-floor sitting area, with the floor-to-ceiling bookcase and the beautiful room divider, also has its own mystery. The apartment is large, but narrow, with an enfilade of rooms taking you into constantly changing atmospheres. Of this inspiring variety – pure visual pleasure – we can only be jealous. If you are afraid of contamination and fearful of decoration, you will miss the beauty of this spot.

De blauwe zitkamer-bibliotheek van Barnaba Fornasetti, met de schitterende paravent geschilderd door zijn vader Piero. Piero Fornasetti hield niet alleen van opulente decoraties, maar ook van forse kleuren. Bijna elk vertrek kreeg een ander kleurbad. Piero gebruikte deze kamer ook als bureau en atelier.

Le séjour-bibliothèque bleu de Barnaba Fornasetti avec le superbe paravent peint par son père Piero. Ne privilégiant pas seulement les décorations opulentes, Piero Fornasetti aimait aussi beaucoup les couleurs vives. Ainsi, presque chacun des espaces se retrouve baigné d'une autre couleur. Cette pièce servait aussi de bureau et d'atelier à Piero.

Barnaba Fornasetti's blue sitting room-library, with its superb folding screen painted by his father Piero. Piero Fornasetti loved not only opulent décors, but also strong colours. Almost every room had its own different colour. Piero used this room also as an office and workshop.

In de slaapkamer waan je je al half in de hemel, tussen de frêle Charivari-stoelen, de typische Fornasetti-commode, het smeedijzeren bed en de wervelende wolken van het behang. In dit huis heeft elk object een ziel en voel je overal de aanwezigheid van de meester, die rechtsonder opduikt.

Entre les chaises Charivari toutes frêles, la commode Fornasetti on ne peut plus caractéristique, le lit en fer forgé et les nuages virevoltants du papier peint, on se croirait dans cette chambre à mi-chemin du ciel. Dans cette maison, le moindre objet a une âme et on sent partout la présence du maître apparaissant ici en bas à droite.

In the bedroom you imagine yourself already halfway to heaven, between the frail Charivari chairs, the typical Fornasetti chest of drawers, the wrought iron bed and the swirling clouds of the wallpaper. In this house every object has a soul and you sense everywhere the presence of the master, who pops up to the lower right.

Het behang in de gang laat ons allerlei zichten op Jeruzalem zien, uiteraard in zwart-wit, waar Piero van hield. Overal merk je zijn met metafysische decors bedrukte borden op. Helemaal rechts zien we een van de wondermooie stoelen, de 'Musicale', ontworpen in 1951 en sinds 2000 weer in productie.

Le papier peint du couloir propose une profusion de vues sur Jérusalem, en noir et blanc comme Piero les préférait. On remarque partout ses assiettes imprimées de décors métaphysiques. Tout à fait à droite, une des merveilleuses chaises, la 'Musicale', créée en 1951 et remise en production depuis 2000.

The wallpaper in the hallway shows views of Jerusalem, a city Piero loved, from all angles, in black and white of course. Everywhere you see wall plates printed with metaphysical decors. At the right we see one of the beautiful chairs, the 'Musicale', designed in 1951 and in production again since 2000.

Barnaba Fornasetti, eveneens ontwerper, woont en werkt in dit hemelse pand en heeft met heruitgaven en nieuwe edities ook het design van zijn vader nieuw leven ingeblazen. Hiernaast bewonderen we een van de meest creatieve en ongewone hoeken van de woning, met het gele constructivistische bureau over-rompeld door souvenirs, een plek waar Piero graag werkte en veel inspiratie vond.

Barnaba Fornasetti, lui-même styliste, habite et travaille dans cette demeure divine. Il a également offert une nouvelle vie au design de son père par le biais de rééditions et de nouvelles publications. Admirons ci-contre un des coins les plus créatifs et insolites de cette maison, avec le bureau entièrement construc-tiviste envahi de souvenirs, un endroit dans lequel Piero se retirait volontiers pour travailler et où il puisait beaucoup d'inspiration.

Barnaba Fornasetti, also a designer, lives and works in this divine property. He has also given a new impetus to his father's design with reprints and new editions. On the facing page we admire one of the most creative and unusual corners of the house, with the yellow constructivist office overwhelmed by souvenirs, a place where Piero loved working and found much of his inspiration.

SIXTIES

ORIGINELE INGREEP

Alleen de huid van dit Antwerpse herenhuis stamt nog uit 1913. Binnen wandel je grotendeels door een hedendaagse creatie. Het pand laat ons een unieke manier van wonen zien, die oud en nieuw op een verrassende wijze met elkaar laat versmelten. De eclectische voorgevel en een aantal stucplafonds bleven bewaard. Maar het interieur werd in de jaren zeventig grondig verbouwd door architect Werner De Bondt, die het in de geest van het modernisme een tussenverdiep schonk. Zo ontstond er een soort podium waarop de toenmalige bewoonster piano kon spelen. Dit architectuurexperiment blijft boeien en was voor de huidige bewoner, Johan Lenaerts, een leidraad om deze moderne lijn door te zetten in de gehele woonruimte. Hij heeft agenturen voor verschillende bekende designmerken. Hij komt ook uit een geslacht van interieurarchitecten en groeide zelf op te midden van modern design. Johan heeft het pand samen met tuinarchitect Dirk Buytaert gerenoveerd en aangekleed. Architect Pascal François stond in voor de nieuwe ingrepen. Hij verruimde de woonkeuken met een groot venster en terras, opgevat als een exterieure living room. Getrouw aan de verbouwing van vroeger kwam er weer overal vasttapijt en rijstpapier op de muren. We merken wat vintagemeubilair op, onder meer van Hans Wegner, lampen van Stilnovo en keramiek van Perignem. De bewoners vinden de combinatie van oud en nieuw, van vintage en actueel design spannend en tijdloos.

INTERVENTION ORIGINALE

Seule l'écorce de cette maison de maître anversoise date encore de 1913. À l'intérieur, on se balade essentiellement dans une création contemporaine. Cette demeure présente une manière d'habiter unique, fusionnant de façon surprenante l'ancien et le neuf. La façade éclectique et quelques plafonds en stuc ont été conservés. Mais l'intérieur a été profondément rénové dans les années 1970 par l'architecte Werner De Bondt qui y intégra, tout à fait dans l'esprit du modernisme, un entresol. C'est ainsi que s'est formée une sorte d'estrade sur laquelle l'occupante de l'époque pouvait jouer du piano. Cette expérience architecturale demeure passionnante et a été pour l'occupant actuel, Johan Lenaerts, un fil conducteur pour étendre cette ligne moderne à tout l'espace de vie. Issu d'une lignée d'architectes d'intérieur et ayant lui-même grandi au milieu de design moderne, Johan Lenaerts a plusieurs agences de diverses célèbres marques de design. Il a rénové et décoré cette propriété avec la collaboration de l'architecte paysager Dirk Buytaert, tandis que l'architecte Pascal François a assumé les nouvelles interventions. Il a notamment agrandi la cuisine américaine d'une grande fenêtre et d'une terrasse conçue comme un séjour extérieur. Dans la ligne de la rénovation antérieure, les sols retrouvèrent la moquette et les murs le papier de riz. On observe, par exemple, quelques meubles vintage de Hans Wegner, des lampes de Stilnovo et des céramiques de Perignem. Pour les habitants actuels, la combinaison d'ancien et de neuf, de vintage et de design actuel est tout aussi intemporelle que passionnante.

ORIGINAL SURGERY

Only the skin of this Antwerp mansion dates from 1913. Inside you walk through what is a largely contemporary creation. The property testifies to a unique way of living, in a surprising blend of old and new. The eclectic front façade and a number of stucco ceilings remain preserved. But the interior was thoroughly transformed in the '70s by architect Werner De Bondt, who in the spirit of modernism put in an intermediate floor, creating a kind of stage on which the former occupant could play the piano. This architectural experiment remains exciting. It also led the current occupant, Johan Lenaerts, to continue the modern line across the entire living area. Johan has agencies for several well-known designer brands. He also comes from a family of interior architects and grew up surrounded by modern design. He has renovated and decorated the property together with landscape architect Dirk Buytaert.

Architect Pascal François was responsible for the further changes, expanding the kitchen-living room with a large window and with a terrace conceived as an exterior living room. True to the earlier renovation, carpet and rice paper again cover the walls. We notice vintage furniture from, among others, Hans Wegner, along with Stilnovo lamps and Perignem ceramics. The residents find the combination of old and new, vintage and contemporary design exciting and timeless.

In het hoge neoklassieke salon met het stucplafond bracht architect Werner De Bondt een tussenverdieping aan, net een balkon van waar je de muziek kon beluisteren die beneden werd gespeeld. Voor Johan Lenaerts is dit een bijzondere plek om zijn meubels te laten zien, ook al door het onwezenlijke licht.

Vu la hauteur du plafond en stuc dans ce salon néoclassique, l'architecte Werner De Bondt a fait aménager un niveau intermédiaire, comme un balcon où on s'installait à l'époque pour écouter la musique jouée en bas. Avec la complicité d'une lumière irréelle, c'est pour Johan Lenaerts un endroit particulier pour présenter ses meubles.

In the high-ceilinged neoclassical salon, architect Werner De Bondt inserted a balcony from where you could listen to the music being played down below. For Johan Lenaerts, this is a special place to show his furniture, also with its unreal light.

Zicht vanuit de tussenverdieping op het podium, waarop ooit een piano stond. Johan Lenaerts sluit zich niet op in een bepaalde stijl of periode en mengt ook moeiteloos hedendaagse creaties met vintage. Het schilderij is van zijn zus Liesbet Lenaerts.

Vue à partir de l'entresol sur l'estrade où s'est trouvé jadis un piano. Loin de s'enfermer dans un style ou une époque définis, Johan Lenaerts mélange sans problème des créations contemporaines avec du vintage. Le tableau est l'œuvre de sa sœur Liesbet Lenaerts.

View from the balcony to the stage on which a piano once stood. Johan Lenaerts does not enclose himself in a particular style or period and effortlessly blends contemporary creations with vintage. The painting is by his sister Liesbet Lenaerts.

Johan is tuk op de meubelontwerpen van
Hans Wegner. De prachtige zetel (achter
in de benedenkamer), de Flag Halyard uit
1950, is zijn pronkstuk.
De moderne invulling schenkt dit interieur
een bijzondere dynamiek en bewijst wat je
allemaal kunt aanvangen onder een hoog
plafond. Let ook op de combinatie van de
oude architectuur met vintage, zoals de
metalen Scoliari-lamp in de gang.

Johan raffole du style de meubles de
Hans Wegner. Le superbe fauteuil
(au fond de la pièce en bas), le Flag
Halyard de 1950, est sa pièce maîtresse.
L'habillage moderne confère à cet
intérieur une dynamique particulière et
illustre bien ce qu'il est possible de faire
sous un haut plafond. Remarquons aussi
la combinaison de l'architecture ancienne
avec le vintage, p. ex. avec la lampe
Scoliari en métal dans le couloir.

Johan is keen on the furniture designs by
Hans Wegner. The beautiful chair (back
of the lower room), the Flag Halyard
from 1950, is his showpiece. The modern
interpretation gives the interior a special
dynamic and proves just how much
scope a high ceiling gives you. Note the
combination of older architecture with
vintage, like the metal Scoliari lamp in
the hallway.

GALLERY

ACTUEEL KUNSTKABINET

De wijze waarop in deze woning architectuur, design en beeldende kunst vergroeien tot één geheel is brandend actueel. Het gebouw in het centrum van havenstad Antwerpen herbergt de woning van Veerle Wenes, haar partner Bob Christiaens en haar galerie 'Valerie Traan'. De benaming van de galerie is een letterspielerei van haar naam. Het is geen designgalerie, maar er zijn wel vrij veel designers te gast die in puur design actief zijn en de grenzen van de actuele beeldende kunst aftasten. Zo bracht Veerle onder meer expo's van Studio Simple, Bram Boo, Fien Muller, Hannes Van Severen, Diane Steverlynck & co en 5IN4E. Maar ook de architecten De Vylder, Vinck en Taillieu en Serge Vandenhove waren er te gast. De tentoonstellingen worden altijd opgebouwd rond een thema, waarin kunst, design en architectuur gemengd worden. De woning en de galerie vormen samen een hedendaags kunstenkabinet. Het pand ligt trouwens naast het Jordaenshuis. Het werd in 1979 een eerste maal verbouwd door architect Eric De Vocht, die de grote, strakke lijnen van de galerie ontwierp. Het werd onlangs door architect Bart Lens helemaal heringericht, waarbij hij zich vooral concentreerde op de woonvleugel. De woning wordt slechts door een glazen binnendeur van de galerie gescheiden. Veerle wil immers dicht bij haar bezoekers en kunstenaars leven. Deze laatsten komen vaak over de vloer om aan de grote eettafel te eten, te drinken en te discussieren. Voor haar is een galerie runnen dan ook een passie. Ook de woonruimte met de grote haard is verrassend monumentaal. Deze ruimte heeft nog typisch zestiende-eeuwse proporties.

UN CABINET DES ARTS ACTUEL

La manière dont l'architecture, le design et les arts plastiques s'unissent dans cette demeure en un seul ensemble est d'une actualité brûlante. Cet édifice au centre de la ville portuaire d'Anvers abrite la demeure de Veerle Wenes, son partenaire Bob Christiaens, ainsi que sa galerie, baptisée d'après un jeu de mots sur son nom, Valerie Traan. Si ce n'est pas véritablement une galerie de design, elle accueille néanmoins de nombreux designers actifs dans le domaine du design pur et explorateurs des frontières des arts plastiques actuels. C'est ainsi que Veerle a organisé des expositions de Studio Simple, Bram Boo, Fien Muller, Hannes Van Severen, Diane Steverlynck & co et 5IN4E. Mais on a pu y rencontrer aussi les architectes De Vylder, Vinck et Taillieu et Serge Vandenhove. Les expositions sont toujours basées sur un thème, avec un mélange d'art, de design et d'architecture. L'habitation et la galerie forment ensemble un cabinet des arts actuel qui est d'ailleurs en bonne compagnie puisqu'il jouxte la Maison Jordaens. La maison a été transformée une première fois en 1979 par l'architecte Eric De Vocht qui a conçu les grandes lignes tendues de la galerie. Beaucoup plus récemment, l'architecte Bart Lens l'a complètement réaménagée en se concentrant davantage sur la partie habitation qui n'est plus séparée de la galerie que par une simple porte en verre. Veerle se soucie en effet de vivre à proximité de ses visiteurs et des artistes. Ces derniers le lui rendent d'ailleurs bien en venant fréquemment s'attabler à sa grande table pour y manger un bout, boire un coup et discuter. On sent bien que la direction d'une galerie est pour elle

une véritable passion. On se laisse encore surprendre par la monumentalité du séjour qui, avec sa grande cheminée, témoigne des proportions caractéristiques du XVIᵉ siècle.

CONTEMPORARY ART COLLECTION

In this home, architecture, design and art fuse into a single whole in very topical way. The building in the centre of the port city of Antwerp is home to Veerle Wenes, her partner Bob Christiaens and her gallery, Valerie Traan (the gallery's name is a word play on her name). It is not a design gallery per se, but it does play host to quite a few designers who are active in pure design and test the borders of contemporary visual art. Veerle has exhibited, for example, Studio Simple, Bram Boo, Fien Muller, Hannes van Severen, Diane Steverlynck & co and 5IN4E. But architects De Vylder, Vinck and Taillieu and Serge Vandenhove have also been guests. The exhibitions are always thematic, with a mix of art, design and architecture. The house and the gallery together form a contemporary art collection. The property, close to the Jordaens House, was converted for the first time in 1979 by architect Eric De Vocht, who drew the gallery's large, clean lines. It recently underwent a makeover by architect Bart Lens, concentrated more on the living wing. The living area is separated from the gallery by a simple glass inner door. Veerle wants to live close to her visitors and artists. The latter often cross the floor to the big table to eat, drink and discuss. For her, running a gallery is a passion. The living room with its large fireplace also is surprisingly monumental. This space retains typically sixteenth-century proportions.

De basisstructuur van de galerie kwam al in 1979 tot stand na een verbouwing door architect Eric De Vocht. Hij tekende onder meer de betonnen trap, die de ruimte domineert. Maar het volledige ensemble werd opnieuw gekneed door architect Bart Lens, een meester in dergelijke renovaties. Dit is de centrale expositieruimte met daarachter de binnentuin en rechts de woning.

Le structure de base de la galerie date de 1979 lors d'une transformation par l'architecte Eric De Vocht qui dessina entre autres l'escalier en béton qui domine nettement l'espace. Mais l'ensemble complet a été remodelé par l'architecte Bart Lens, véritable maître de ce genre de rénovations. Voici l'espace d'exposition central, avec derrière le jardin clos et à droite la maison.

The basic structure of the gallery already came into being in 1979 with its conversion by architect Eric De Vocht. He signed, among other things, the concrete staircase that dominates the space. But the whole ensemble was later remoulded by architect Bart Lens, who is a master in such renovations. This is the central exhibition space with behind the patio and to the right the apartment.

VIDE-
GRENIER

VIDE-GRENIER

Je hoeft een simpel rijhuis met een traditioneel grondplan niet open te breken om er iets bijzonders van te maken. Misschien juist zelfs niet, legt Frederika Laloo uit, die in Brugge, samen met haar man John Hinderyckx, een gezellig pand vol leuke trouvailles bewoont. Om de leefruimte te actualiseren, wordt de achterbouw meestal gesloopt en vervangen door een glazen wand. Maar dan wordt de intimiteit verbroken. Dit pand bestaat uit talrijke kamertjes die de juiste proporties hebben en telkens anders werden aangekleed. Het pand is niet groot, maar werd door deze aankleding enorm verruimd en blijkt overal leefhoeken te herbergen. John en Frederika verzamelen al heel lang vintage. 'Al van toen moderne spullen uit de jaren vijftig en zestig gewoon werden weggegooid', vertelt Frederika. Liefst struinen ze vlooienmarkten af in Midden-Frankrijk. 'Op zo'n *vide-grenier* vind je van alles en krijg je soms ook de kans om even binnen te gluren in oude huizen, wat het zoeken extra spannend maakt. Bovendien lopen er in de Franse binnenlanden amper toeristen rond', merkt Frederika op. Boven in de woning bouwde ze ook een gastenkamer, van waaruit je een schitterend uitzicht hebt over de oude stad. John en Frederika logeren soms ook zelf in hun eigen gastenflat en gaan zo een beetje op reis in eigen huis. De woning baadt in een warme gloed door de leuke kleuren die elke kamer sieren. Kleur versterkt de intimiteit en geeft elke ruimte een identiteit. Maar overal zijn de plinten en deuren wit geborsteld, wat de algemene harmonie van het interieur versterkt.

VIDE-GRENIER

Dans une simple maison mitoyenne au plan traditionnel, il n'est pas toujours nécessaire de casser des murs pour en faire quelque chose de particulier. « C'est peut-être précisément ce qu'il ne faut pas faire », explique Frederika Laloo qui habite avec son mari John Hinderyckx une agréable maison pleine de trouvailles à Bruges. En général, afin d'actualiser l'espace de vie, l'arrière-maison est démolie et remplacée par une paroi en verre. Mais de cette façon, on supprime aussi l'intimité. Cette maison se compose de nombreuses petites pièces de proportions agréables et toutes décorées de manière différente. Si la maison n'est pas grande, cette décoration la rend nettement plus spacieuse et elle abrite un peu partout des espaces de vie. John et Frederika collectionnent du vintage depuis fort longtemps. « Déjà depuis l'époque où on jetait tout simplement les trucs modernes des années cinquante et soixante », raconte Frederika. Ils adorent faire les marchés aux puces dans le centre de la France. « On trouve de tout dans ces vide-greniers et parfois, on a même l'occasion de jeter un coup d'œil dans d'anciennes demeures et cela rend les recherches encore plus passionnantes. En plus, il y a à peine quelques touristes à l'intérieur du pays en France », ajoute encore Frederika. En haut de la maison, elle a aménagé une chambre d'hôte avec une très belle vue vie sur le cœur historique de la ville. Parfois, John et Frederika logent eux-mêmes dans leur propre chambre d'hôte et partent ainsi en voyage dans leur propre maison. Une maison baignée de chaude lumière grâce aux couleurs de chacune des chambres qui en augmentent l'intimité et lui confèrent une identité propre. Mais en même temps, toutes les plinthes et les portes sont peintes en blanc, assurant ainsi une harmonie générale à cet intérieur.

VIDE-GRENIER

If you have a simple terraced town house with a traditional floorplan, there is no need to start breaking down walls to make something special out of it. Perhaps this is precisely what you shouldn't do, explains Frederika Laloo, who with her husband John Hinderyckx lives in a cosy house in Bruges full of amusing *trouvailles*. To update the living space the standard solution is to demolish the rear of the building and replace it with a glass wall. But then the sense of intimacy is gone. This house consists of lots of small rooms, beautifully proportioned and each decorated differently. The building is not big, but they way it is decorated enlarges it enormously, with 'living corners' all over the place. John and Frederika have been collecting vintage for many years. "Ever since modern stuff from the '50s and '60s started to be normally thrown away", says Frederika. Their favourite occupation is roaming flea markets in central France. "At such *vide-greniers* full of objects from emptied houses, you can find anything and everything. And with a bit of luck you can sometimes take a peek inside old houses, which makes the searching even more exciting. Moreover in the centre of France you find only tourists", Frederika notes. At the top of the house they have also built a guest room, where visitors have a wonderful view over the old town. John and Frederika sometimes stay in their own guest apartment and go travelling as guests in their own house. The house is bathed in the warm glow of the pleasant colours that decorate every room. Colour enhances the sense of intimacy and gives each room its own identity. But everywhere the baseboards and doors are brush painted white, adding to the general harmony of the interior.

De oude woonkamer werd gewoon rood geschilderd en lekker vol-gestouwd met leuke vondsten. Maar aan de architectuur zelf werd niets veranderd. De bewoners houden van hun oude pand met de talrijke kamers, maar gaven het interieur een moder-nere swing.

L'ancien séjour a été simplement repeint en rouge et joyeusement rempli de trouvailles plaisantes, tandis que l'architecture n'a en rien été modifiée. Les habitants adorent leur vieille demeure avec ses nombreuses pièces, mais ils ont pourvu l'intérieur d'un swing plus moderne.

The old living room was just painted red and tastily packed with great finds. But no changes were made to the architecture itself. The occupants love their old building with its many rooms, but gave the interior a more modern swing.

Elke kamer heeft een ander verhaal en tint. Dit is een kleine meditatieruimte boven, waar ook de laptop staat. Het is een beetje een charmante stapelruimte, stijlvol en intiem. De bewoners hebben ook bijna alles zelf opgeknapt. Het houten reliëf aan de muur is een creatie van John, die ook vintage fietsen verzamelt en herstelt.

Chacune des pièces baigne dans un autre ton et raconte une autre histoire. Voici un petit espace de méditation à l'étage, où se trouve aussi l'ordinateur portable. C'est en quelque sorte un espace de rangement charmant, stylé et intime. Les habitants ont d'ailleurs quasiment tout retapé eux-mêmes. Le relief en bois au mur est l'œuvre de John qui collectionne et répare par ailleurs des bicyclettes vintage.

Each room has a different story and hue. This is a small meditation room upstairs, where the laptop sits. It has something of a charming warehouse about it, stylish and intimate. The residents have refurbished almost everything themselves. The wooden relief on the wall is a creation of John who also collects and restores vintage bicycles.

COUNTRY

MONUMENT

Deze oude hoeve bij Hilvarenbeek, in de Nederlandse Kempen, leidt een nieuw leven als woonatelier. Het gebouw stamt uit 1870 en wordt landschappelijk als een monument beschouwd, waardoor de straatgevel perfect moest worden gerestaureerd. In ruil voor deze opknapbeurt mocht architect Wim De Vos wel het hele interieur op een hedendaagse wijze aanpassen en de achtergevel openen naar de tuin, die werd ontworpen door Ludovic Devriendt. Het oude dakspant bleef bewaard en rust nu op een stalen structuur. De oude indeling bleef bewaard, maar de zoldering ging er uit om een loft te creëren die open is tot aan de nok. De Vos zorgde voor de sobere structuren, bewoner Arnold Otten en zijn vriend John Biesheuvel voor de aankleding en kleuren. De grote ruimte werd zo het woonatelier van beeldend kunstenaar Biesheuvel die, net als zijn grote voorbeeld Madeleine Castaing, tuk is op zwart Napoleon III-meubilair. In het Italiaanse Charivari vonden ze de zwarte vederlichte stoelen die je overal in dit interieur tegenkomt. In de woonruimte worden wonen, werken en vrienden ontvangen moeiteloos met elkaar gecombineerd. Enkele ruwe meubels en onafgewerkte fauteuils zorgen voor een extra artistieke toets. Afgewerkt zouden deze meubels te burgerlijk ogen voor dit interieur. Boeiend is ook het contrast tussen de open ruimte en de gesloten keuken in de oude vleugel van de boerderij, tussen geschiedenis en hedendaagse wooncultuur.

MONUMENT

This old farmhouse near Hilvarenbeek, in the Dutch Kempen, has taken on a new life as a live-in studio. The building, dating from 1870, is a listed landscape monument, requiring the street façade to be perfectly restored. In exchange for putting this to rights, architect Wim De Vos was allowed to adapt the entire interior in a contemporary fashion and to open the rear wall onto the garden, designed by Ludovic Devriendt. The old roof frame was preserved and now rests on a steel structure. The original layout was preserved, but the ceiling disappeared to create a loft that is open to the rafters. De Vos provided the austere structures and resident Arnold Otten and his friend John Biesheuvel the decoration and colours. The large space became in this way the live-in studio of artist Biesheuvel who, like his great example Madeleine Castaing, loves black Napoleon III furniture. In the Italian Charivari they found the black lightweight chairs that you find everywhere in the interior. In the living area, living, working and entertaining friends are effortlessly combined. Some rough furniture and unfinished armchairs provide an extra artistic touch. Finished, they would look too bourgeois for this interior. Also fascinating is the contrast between the open space and the closed kitchen in the old wing of the farm, between history and contemporary living culture.

MONUMENT

Cette ancienne ferme près de la Hilvarenbeek dans la Campine hollandaise a trouvé une nouvelle destination et tant qu'atelier et habitation. Datant de 1870, la demeure est considérée comme monument paysager et la façade côté rue a donc dû être très fidèlement restaurée. En contrepartie, l'architecte Wim De Vos a pu adapter tout l'intérieur aux normes contemporaines comme il a pu ouvrir la façade donnant sur le jardin créé par Ludovic Devriendt. L'ancienne charpente a été conservée mais repose maintenant sur une structure en acier. De même, l'ancienne répartition a également été conservée, mais le plafond a disparu pour créer un loft ouvert jusqu'au faîte du toit. De Vos a conçu les structures sobres tandis que l'occupant Arnold Otten et son ami John Biesheuvel se sont occupés de la décoration et des couleurs. Le grand espace est devenu l'atelier et l'habitation du plasticien Biesheuvel qui adore, à l'instar de son idole Madeleine Castaing, le mobilier noir Napoléon III. Les chaises noires d'une grande légèreté qu'on trouve partout dans cet intérieur viennent de Charivari en Italie. L'espace de vie permet de combiner aisément l'habitation, le travail et l'accueil des amis. Quelques meubles bruts et des fauteuils inachevés – un mobilier 'fini' aurait ici l'air bien trop bourgeois – procurent une belle touche artistique à cet intérieur. Il est intéressant aussi de voir le contraste entre l'espace ouvert et la cuisine fermée dans l'aile ancienne de la ferme, entre l'histoire et la culture d'habitation contemporaine.

De voorgevel werd perfect hersteld, maar de achtergevel werd opgetrokken. Zo ontwierp architect Wim De Vos een grote leefruimte die tevens als atelier dienstdoet. Het ruimtegevoel en het zicht op de grote tuin zorgen voor een intense architectuurbeleving. Let ook op de originele meubels, deels modern, deels Napoleon III.

La façade a été parfaitement restaurée, mais en rehaussant la façade arrière, l'architecte Wim De Vos a créé un grand espace de vie qui fait également office d'atelier. Ce sens de l'espace et la vue sur le grand jardin procurent une expérience architecturale intense. Observons aussi l'originalité du mobilier, en partie moderne, en partie Napoléon III.

The front façade was precisely restored, but the back wall was built out, giving architect Wim De Vos the space to design a large living room that also serves as a studio. The sense of space and a view of the garden provide an intense architectural experience. Note also the original furniture, part modern and part Napoleon III.

MOLLINO

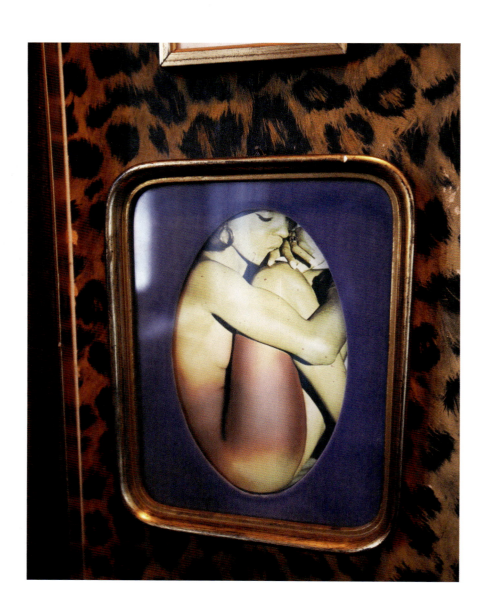

MOLLINO

De Italiaanse ontwerper Carlo Mollino (1905 – 1973) is niet alleen een cultfiguur, hij was ook een beetje occult. Dit is bijvoorbeeld de flat die hij nooit echt heeft bewoond, aldus Fulvio Ferrari, die in Turijn samen met zijn zoon Napoleone de Casa Mollino runt, een privémuseum in een van de voormalige woningen van Mollino. Hij richtte deze flat in, maar heeft er dus nooit geslapen. Na zijn dood werd de flat leeggehaald. Fulvio Ferrari heeft hem vervolgens verworven, helemaal heringericht en gered. De basiselementen, zoals de door Mollino ontworpen schouw, de Japanse schuifdeuren en de betegeling van badkamer en keuken bleven gelukkig bewaard. Via oude vrienden van Mollino slaagde Ferrari erin om allerlei meubels, objecten en foto's terug te brengen. Zo heeft hij ook alles weer perfect kunnen reconstrueren. De slaapkamer is een ode aan de faraonische Egyptische architect Kha, waar Mollino een grote belangstelling voor had. Op de wanden prijken ontelbare vlinders, die voor de Egyptenaren symbolen waren van het geluk. De flat heeft een uitgesproken intiem karakter en de living room lijkt op een boudoir en herinnert qua stijl zeker aan het wonderbaarlijke Teatro Regio, dat hij in 1973 in Turijn mocht optrekken. Mollino, die niet alleen gebouwen ontwierp, maar ook sensueel meubilair en racewagens, was eveneens de auteur van prachtige erotische foto's waarvan de decors doen denken aan deze flat op de oever van de Po. Dit appartement wordt trouwens het best bezocht tegen valavond, wanneer het licht de intimiteit nog versterkt.

MOLLINO

Italian designer and cult figure Carlo Mollino (1905 – 1973) also dabbled in the occult. This is for example the flat he never really lived in, says Fulvio Ferrari who runs the Casa Mollino in Turin with his son Napoleone. It is a private museum of Mollino in one of his former homes. Mollino furnished this flat, but never slept in it. After his death, the flat was emptied. Fulvio Ferrari then acquired it, completely refurbished and saved it. The basic elements were fortunately preserved, such as the fireplace that Mollino designed, the Japanese sliding doors and the bathroom and kitchen tiling. With the help of old friends of Mollino, Ferrari succeeded in gathering back all kinds of furniture, objects and photos, enabling him to do a perfect reconstruction job. The bedroom is an ode to the Pharaonic Egyptian architect Kha who was very important for Mollino. The walls are lined with countless butterflies that were symbols of happiness for the Egyptians. The flat has a distinctly intimate character and the living room looks like a boudoir. Stylistically it immediately calls to mind the wonderful Teatro Regio that Mollino built in Turin in 1973. Mollino designed not only buildings but also sensuous furniture and racing cars. He was also the author of superb erotic pictures with decors reminiscent of this apartment on the banks of the Po. This apartment is best visited at dusk, when the light reinforces the sense of intimacy.

MOLLINO

Le styliste italien Carlo Mollino (1905 – 1973) n'est pas seulement une figure culte, mais il a également été tant soit peu occulte. Voici, par exemple, l'appartement où il n'a jamais habité réellement, selon Fulvio Ferrari qui dirige avec son fils Napoleone la Casa Mollino à Turin. Il s'agit d'un musée privé d'une des anciennes maisons de Mollino. Il a donc bien aménagé cet appartement mais n'y a jamais passé la nuit. Alors que l'habitation a été complètement vidée après sa mort, Fulvio Ferrari a su l'acquérir pour le réaménager entièrement et assurer ainsi sa sauvegarde. Heureusement, les éléments de base ont pu être conservés : ainsi la cheminée dessinée par Mollino ainsi que les portes coulissantes japonaises et la faïence de la cuisine et de la salle de bain. Par le biais d'anciens amis de Mollino, Ferrari a pu également ramener divers meubles, objets et photos et a réussi finalement une reconstruction quasiment parfaite. La chambre à coucher est un hommage à l'architecte égyptien pharaonique « kha » auquel Mollino portait une grande admiration. Les parois sont décorées d'innombrables papillons, symboles de bonheur pour les Égyptiens. L'appartement dégage un caractère intime prononcé et avec son air de boudoir, le séjour rappelle par son style le merveilleux Teatro Regio qu'il a pu ériger en 1973 à Turin. Créateur d'édifices mais aussi styliste d'un mobilier sensuel et de voitures de course, Mollino est également l'auteur de superbes photos érotiques dont les décors rappellent cet appartement sur les rives du Po. Il vaut d'ailleurs mieux de visiter cet appartement au crépuscule, quand la lumière renforce encore le caractère d'intimité.

De flat werd na de dood van Carlo Mollino leeggehaald, maar dankzij vader en zoon Ferrari helemaal heringericht, precies zoals het was. Gelukkig bleven tal van decoratieve elementen toch bewaard, zoals de tegels in de excentrieke badkamer. De slaapkamer is een ode aan de faraonische architect Kha, de vele vlinders waren voor de Egyptenaren symbolen van geluk. In deze flat hangt een fascinerende sfeer met een erotische geladenheid en veel intimiteit.

L'appartement avait été vidé après la mort de Carlo Mollino, mais grâce aux Ferrari père et fils, il a été entièrement réaménagé tel qu'il était jadis. Heureusement, de nombreux éléments de la décoration tels que les carreaux dans la salle de bain excentrique, avaient été conservés. Avec ses nombreux papillons, symboles de bonheur pour les Égyptiens, la chambre à coucher est un hommage à l'architecte Kha de l'époque pharaonique. Cet appartement respire une ambiance fascinante chargée d'érotisme et de beaucoup d'intimité.

The apartment was emptied after Carlo Mollino's death, but thanks to father and son Ferrari completely refurbished just as it was. Luckily, many decorative elements are still preserved, like the tiles in the eccentric bathroom. The bedroom is an ode to the pharaonic architect Kha, the many butterflies were for the Egyptians symbols of happiness. There is a fascinating atmosphere in this flat, full of erotic tension and lots of intimacy.

BOX

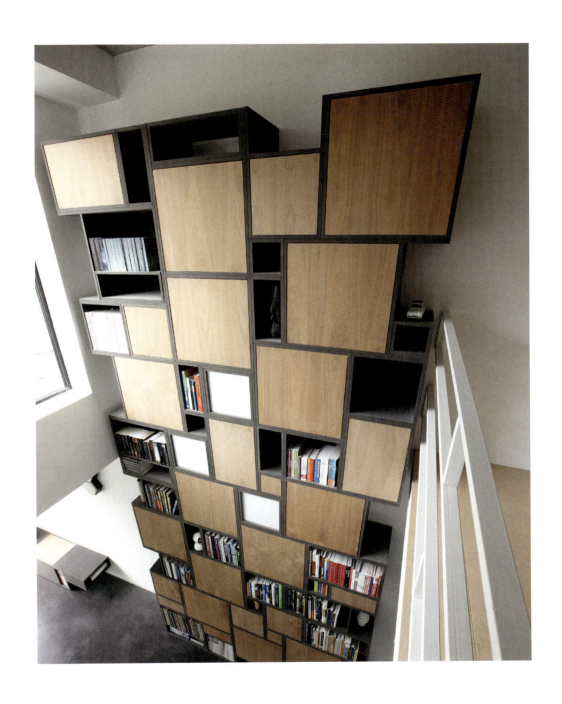

Meubelontwerper Filip Janssens leeft in een grote open ruimte met kookhoek, werkhoek, zithoek en eethoek, waarvan de onderdelen deels door zelf ontworpen kasten worden gescheiden. Midden in deze ruimte staat een twee verdiepingen hoge modulaire kast, opgebouwd uit aparte verplaatsbare dozen. Deze kast is echt bedacht als een gebouw. Maar ook de kleine kast ernaast heeft een hoog architectuurgehalte.

Le créateur de mobilier Filip Janssens vit dans un grand espace ouvert avec un coin cuisine, un coin de travail, un coin salon et salle à manger, dont les différentes parties se trouvent partiellement séparées par des armoires créées par lui. Au milieu de l'espace s'élève une armoire modulaire sur deux étages, composée de boîtes distinctes qu'il est possible de déplacer. Si la construction est réellement conçue comme un édifice, la petite armoire à côté possède également un niveau architectural très élevé.

Furniture designer Filip Janssens lives in a large open space with kitchen, work area, lounge and dining area, the different parts of which are partly separated off by self-designed cupboards. In the middle of this room is a two-storey modular cupboard composed of separate boxes that can be moved around. This cupboard is conceived like a building. But the small cabinet next to it also has a high architectural content.

Filip heeft een patent op compacte constructies. Kijk bijvoorbeeld naar de wandkast in zijn tuinpaviljoen of naar de diagonale commode. Zelfs de woning lijkt binnenin op een compositie van op elkaar gestapelde dozen.

Les constructions compactes sont désormais la spécialité de Filip. Voyons, par exemple, le placard dans son chalet de jardin ou la commode diagonale. Même l'ensemble intérieur de la maison a l'air d'une composition de boîtes entassées l'une sur l'autre.

Filip's speciality is compact constructions. Look, for example, at the wardrobe in his garden pavilion or the diagonal chest of drawers. The apartment inside looks like a composition of stacked boxes.

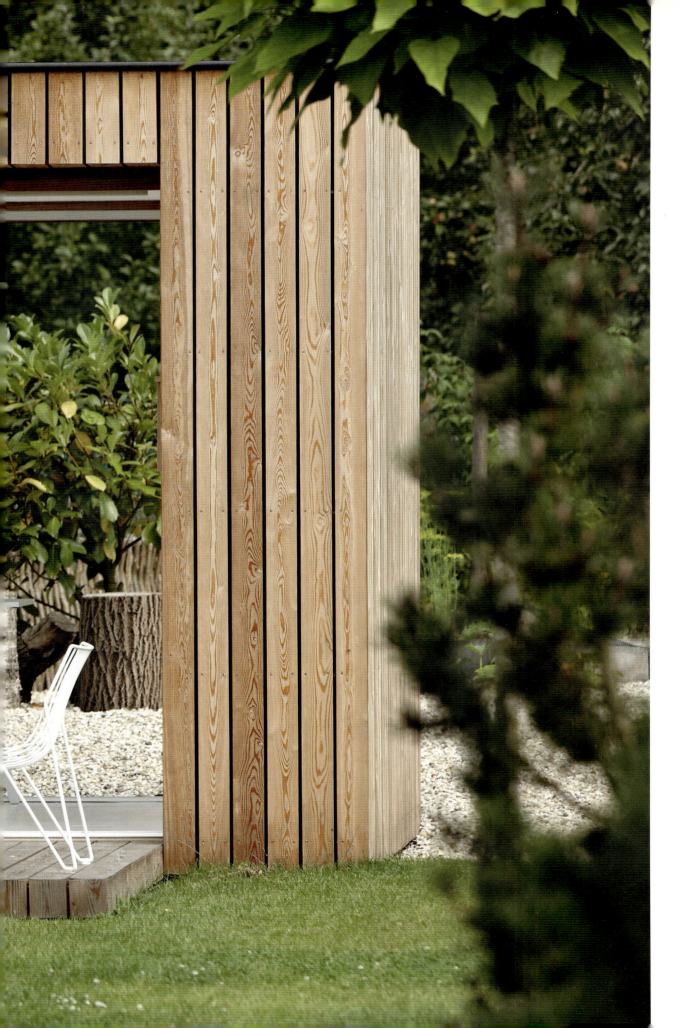

In de tuin kwam er een apart
paviljoen, helemaal opgetrokken
uit hout. Dit is de zomerkamer
van het huis. Eenmaal de twee
ramen openstaan, is het gebouw
weinig meer dan een luifel waar
je zelfs op een regenachtig
moment onder kunt schuilen.

Dans le jardin se trouve un chalet
séparé entièrement construit en
bois. C'est la pièce d'été de la
maison car une fois les fenêtres
ouvertes, il ne reste guère plus
qu'un auvent mais qui offre un
abri parfait même quand il pleut.

In the garden came a separate
pavilion, built completely of
wood. This is the summer room
of the house. Once the two
windows are open, the building is
little more than a canopy offering
shelter during a rain shower.

VINTAGE

ZIEL EN SLIJTAGE

Vintage-antiquair Frederic Hooft richt graag huizen in. Meestal gaat het om hedendaagse woningen. Maar zelf betrekt hij een eeuwenoud huis in de historische binnenstad van Gent. Hij houdt van het kloppend hart van de stad en is ook tuk op oude gebouwen. Een loft vindt hij zelf te modieus, zo'n oud huis met een kronkelende trap en vele kamers met oude planken vloeren vindt hij verrassender. Zijn huis is minstens vier eeuwen oud. Op de moerbalken staan fraaie renaissancemotieven. Ook de circulatie maakt deze woning interessant. De spiltrap vooraan leidt je via een passerelle naar het achterhuis, waar zijn vriendin, Eva Goethals, haar grafische studio heeft. Door alle kamers te benutten als woon- en werkruimte én de circulatie hebben ze de indruk een heel groot pand te bewonen. Ook hier is de tuin een extra woonkamer. Het huis werd zacht hersteld en oude, versleten elementen bleven bewaard, zoals de piepende deurtjes en het afgebladderde plafond, dat bijzonder schilderachtig is. Let ook op het prachtige vintage meubilair van onder meer Jean Prouvé, Alvar Aalto, Willy Van Der Meeren en Lucien Ingels. De collectie van Frederic is groot en erg smaakvol gekozen. Hij combineert vintage met antieke Oosterse tapijten. Kijk ook naar de industriële keuken die beneden staat: simpel, handig en mooi. De woning heeft veel van een artistieke studio die ietwat onaf is, wat de dynamische sfeer versterkt.

L'ÂME ET L'USURE

L'antiquaire de vintage Frederic Hooft adore aménager des maisons. Il s'agit la plupart du temps de maisons contemporaines, mais lui-même habite une maison séculaire dans le centre historique de Gand. Il aime le battement du cœur de la ville tout comme les maisons anciennes. Estimant qu'un loft est trop à la mode, il préfère les surprises d'une maison ancienne avec un escalier en colimaçon et de nombreuses pièces au vieux plancher grinçant. Sa propre maison a plus de quatre siècles, ce dont témoignent les jolis motifs renaissance sur les poutres maîtresses. La circulation dans la maison la rend intéressante aussi. L'escalier à noyau plein à l'avant conduit par une passerelle vers la partie arrière de la maison où se situe l'atelier graphique de son amie Eva Goethals. Grâce à l'utilisation de toutes les pièces comme lieux de vie et de travail et à la circulation, ils ont l'impression d'habiter une maison immense. En plus, ici aussi le jardin sert de salle de séjour supplémentaire. La maison a subi une réhabilitation douce, avec maintien d'anciens éléments usés comme les petites portes grinçantes ou la peinture écaillée du plafond qui donne un effet très pictural. On remarque aussi les superbes meubles vintage de gens comme Jean Prouvé, Alvar Aalto, Willy Van Der Meeren et Lucien Ingels. L'importante collection de Frederic témoigne de son goût raffiné. Il combine d'ailleurs le vintage avec d'anciens tapis d'Orient. La cuisine industrielle en bas mérite aussi toute notre attention : elle est en même temps simple, pratique et belle. La demeure a un côté artistique qui parait inachevé, ce qui renforce l'ambiance dynamique.

SOUL AND WEAR AND TEAR

Vintage antique dealer Frederic Hooft enjoys designing house interiors. These are usually in contemporary homes. He himself, however, inhabits a centuries-old house in the historic centre of Ghent. He loves both the beating heart of the city and old buildings. A loft he finds overly fashionable. For him an old house with a twisting staircase and lots of rooms with old wooden floorboards offers more surprises. His home is at least four centuries old. Charming Renaissance motifs decorate the tie-beams. The traffic patterns also add to the interest of this home. The spiral staircase to the front leads, via a footbridge, to the rear house where his friend Eva Goethals has her graphic studio. Using all rooms as living and working space and having this traffic pattern gives the impression of inhabiting a very large building. Here too the garden provides an additional living room. The house has been restored gently, preserving old, worn elements like the squeaky doors and the particularly picturesque flaking ceiling. Note the beautiful vintage furniture, including Jean Prouvé, Alvar Aalto, Willy Van Der Meeren and Lucien Ingels. Frederic's collection is large and very tastefully chosen. Vintage is combined with antique Oriental rugs. Take a peep also at the industrial kitchen downstairs: simple, useful and beautiful. The house feels much like a somewhat unfinished artist's studio, which reinforces the dynamic atmosphere.

In de benedenkamer merk je aan
de oneffen wanden en de prachtige
balken goed hoe oud dit pand wel
is. Tal van oude elementen bleven
bewaard, zoals het afgebladderde
plafond en de vloer. In deze context
past de industriële keuken perfect.
De stoelen aan de tafel van Maarten
Van Severen zijn ontworpen door
Christophe Gevers.

Dans la pièce du bas, on constate
aisément la vétusté de cette demeure,
ne fût-ce que par l'inégalité des murs
et les poutres superbes. D'autres
éléments anciens tels que les sols et
le plafond à la peinture écaillée ont
également été conservés, un contexte
qui convient merveilleusement à la
cuisine industrielle. Les chaises à la
table de Maarten Van Severen sont
une création de Christophe Gevers.

In the downstairs room you notice the
building's age from its uneven walls
and superb beams. Lots of old elements have been preserved, including
the peeling ceiling and the floor. The
industrial kitchen perfectly into such
a context. The chairs at the Maarten
Van Severen table are designed by
Christophe Gevers.

Het huis heeft een intieme binnenkoer met een passerelle die naar het achterhuis leidt. Boven bleven alle vloeren, deuren en schouwen bewaard. De leren zit is van Maarten Van Severen, het boemerangtafeltje ernaast van Willy Van Der Meeren. De antieke houten bankjes zijn een ontwerp van Le Corbusier.

Dans l'intimité de la cour intérieure, une passerelle conduit à l'arrière de la maison. À l'étage, toutes les portes et les cheminées ainsi que les sols ont été conservés. Le siège en cuir est de Maarten Van Severen, la table d'appoint en boumerang à côté de Willy Van Der Meeren. Les petits bancs antiques en bois ont été créés par Le Corbusier.

The house has an intimate inner courtyard with a walkway leading to the building to the rear. Upstairs, all the all floors, doors and fireplaces have been preserved. The leather chair is by Maarten Van Severen, the boomerang table next to it by Willy Van Der Meeren. The antique wood benches were designed by Le Corbusier.

COLLECTOR

De flat van vintagehandelaar en collectioneur Frederic Rozier is een lange ruimte onder het dak. Het is dus een woonzolder en heeft iets van een elegante stapelruimte vol topdesign. Rozier houdt vooral van de jaren zestig en zeventig. Zijn geprefereerde designer is Joe Colombo. De zit- en eethoek worden van de slaaphoek gescheiden door een monumentale paravent van Dino Gavina.

L'appartement du négociant et collectionneur de vintage Frederic Rozier est un espace tout en longueur sous le toit. C'est donc en fait un grenier aménagé en espace de vie qui a quelque chose d'un élégant espace de rangement bondé de design de grande qualité. Son styliste préféré est Joe Colombo. Le coin séjour et salle à manger est séparé du coin chambre à coucher par un paravent monumental créé par Dino Gavina.

Vintage dealer and collector Frederic Rozier's apartment is a long space under the roof. It is a residential attic and has something of an elegant warehouse full of top design. Rozier is particularly keen on the '60s and '70s. His preferred designer is Joe Colombo. The sitting and dining area is separated from the sleeping area by a monumental Dino Gavina screen.

VINTAGE HOUSE

AMPERSAND HOUSE

Je wordt verliefd op een mooi huis en je leven verandert. Dat lot overkwam Kathryn Smith en haar man Ike Udechuku. Ze komen uit Australië, trokken de wereld rond, woonden in New York, San Francisco en Londen. Uiteindelijk vielen ze voor de charme van Brussel, waar ze hun droom realiseerden: een woongalerie. In Brussel ontdekten ze een schitterend herenhuis met veel ruimte dat ze helemaal bewonen, van beneden tot boven, en waarin ze terzelfdertijd een kunst- en vintagegalerie runnen: het Ampersand House. 'Door met je verzameling kunst en design in huis te leven, ontstaat er een heel intense band,' legt Kathryn uit 'en is het leuk om mensen uit te nodigen die voor extra dynamiek zorgen.' Een galeriewoning evolueert constant van inrichting, want soms vinden ze dagelijks iets nieuws. Ze maken amper onderscheid tussen beeldende kunst, design en kunstnijverheid. Voor hen lopen deze disciplines gewoon in elkaar over. In hun woning staat er veel Deens design. Dat waarderen ze omwille van de elegante lijn en het ambachtelijke vakmanschap. Deze meubels werden in de jaren vijftig en zestig niet zelden manueel vervaardigd in kleine ateliers. Dit design, op zich al antiek, blijft actueel van vorm en uitstraling, ook in dit historisch interieur. Maar Kathryn en Ike combineren oud en nieuw, en houden ook van het actueel design van de Belgische designers Nathalie Dewez, Benoît Deneufbourg en Danny Venlet.

AMPERSAND HOUSE

Un coup de foudre pour une belle maison peut changer la vie. C'est ce qui est arrivé à Kathryn Smith et son mari Ike Udechuku. Originaires d'Australie, ils ont bourlingué de par le monde, habitant à New York, San Francisco et Londres. Finalement, ils sont tombés sous le charme de... Bruxelles où ils ont pu réaliser leur rêve : une demeure-galerie. Ils ont en effet découvert à Bruxelles une magnifique maison de maître avec beaucoup d'espace, qu'ils occupent entièrement, de bas en haut, mais où ils tiennent également une galerie d'art et de vintage : Ampersand House. En vivant avec une collection d'art et de design dans la maison, explique Kathryn, il naît un lien très intense et cela fait plaisir d'inviter des gens qui apportent un surplus de dynamisme. Une demeure-galerie fait évoluer constamment son intérieur car il peut arriver qu'on trouve quotidiennement une nouveauté. Ils ne font pas vraiment de distinction entre les arts plastiques, le design et l'artisanat d'art car ils considèrent que ces disciplines débordent l'une dans l'autre. Leur demeure présente beaucoup de design danois qu'ils apprécient pour son élégance et le savoir-faire artisanal. Il n'était pas rare que dans les années cinquante et soixante, ces meubles soient fabriqués à la main dans de petits ateliers. Et même dans cet intérieur historique, ce design qui est en soi antique, demeure actuel par ses formes et son rayonnement. Mais combinant l'ancien et le contemporain, Kathryn et Ike apprécient aussi beaucoup le design actuel de designers belges comme Nathalie Dewez, Benoît Deneufbourg et Danny Venlet.

AMPERSAND HOUSE

You fall in love with a beautiful house and your life changes. That fate befell Kathryn Smith and her husband Ike Udechuku. Coming from Australia, they travelled the world, living in New York, San Francisco and London. Eventually they fell for the charms of Brussels where they are realizing their dream of a gallery home. In Brussels they discovered a magnificent mansion with lots of space that they inhabit completely from top to bottom, and in which they simultaneously run an art and vintage gallery: the Ampersand House. Living in one house with your art and design collection creates a very intense bond, Kathryn explains. It is also it fun to invite people who provide additional dynamism. The furnishings in a home gallery are constantly evolving, because every day you find something new. They make little distinction between art, design and crafts, disciplines that for them overlap and run into each other. Their home contains a lot of Danish design that they appreciate for its elegant lines and traditional craftsmanship. In the '50s and '60s this furniture was often hand-made in small workshops. This design, although already in the antique category, remains contemporary in shape and feel, even in this historic interior. But Kathryn and Ike combine old and new. They also love the current work of Belgian designers Nathalie Dewez, Benoît Deneufbourg and Danny Venlet.

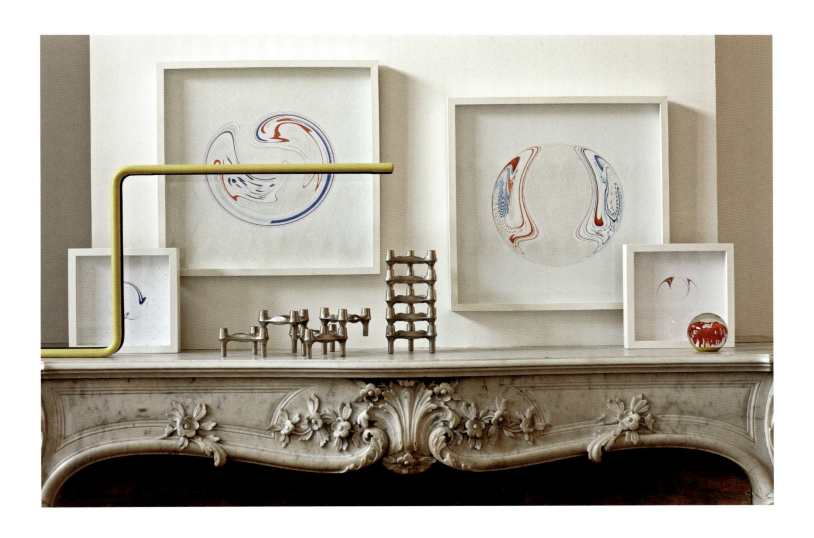

In amper enkele jaren tijd bouwden Kathryn en Ike een internationale reputatie op met hun woongalerie Ampersand House. Het combineren van een art gallery met een woning blijkt heel actueel en aantrekkelijk. Het Ampersand House staat vol prachtig design van onder meer Verner Panton (zigzag), Warren Platner (tafel) en Hans Wegner (houten stoel).

En quelques années à peine, Kathryn et Ike se sont acquis une réputation internationale avec leur demeure-galerie Ampersand House. La combinaison d'une galerie d'art avec une habitation semble en effet très contemporaine et attrayante. Parmi le superbe design abondamment présent dans Ampersand House, observons celui de Verner Planton (zigzag), Warren Platner (table) et Hans Wegner (siège en bois).

In the space of just a few years, Kathryn and Ike built an international reputation with their Ampersand House home-gallery. Combining a art gallery and a home is at once very up-to-date and attractive. Ampersand House is full of wonderful design including Verner Panton (zigzag), Warren Platner (table) and Hans Wegner (wooden chair).

De woning is ook heel aangenaam door haar open structuur en luchtige aankleding met veel witte wanden. Zelfs de inkomhal met de smeedijzeren voordeur is schitterend. Het stoeltje is van de Finse ontwerper Ilmari Tapiovaara.

La maison est aussi très agréable par sa structure ouverte et sa décoration toute en légèreté avec beaucoup de parois blanches. Même le vestibule avec la superbe porte en fer forgé est splendide. La petite chaise est l'œuvre du styliste finlandais Ilmari Tapiovaara.

The house is very pleasant with its open structure and airy décor with lots of white walls. Even the entrance hall with its wrought iron front door is brilliant. The chair is by Finnish designer Ilmari Tapiovaara.

LOFT

DE FABRIEKSLOFT

De noordgrens tussen Frankrijk en België ligt bezaaid met oude textielfabrieken uit de negentiende en de twintigste eeuw. In Kortrijk stappen we een oude spinnerij binnen. Architect Patrick Six heeft er zijn loft en architectuuratelier in ondergebracht. Hij heeft amper aan het gebouw geraakt, maar heeft het exterieur wel in een zwarte jas gehuld. Het complex ziet er vanbuiten gesloten uit, wat de intimiteit van het interieur versterkt. Met zijn bureau 'Ensemble-1' verbouwt Six wel meer oude industriële panden. Hij vertrekt graag van een bestaande en ietwat ongewone structuur. Hier en daar werd een wand doorbroken voor een extra venster. De grote woonruimte bevindt zich in de vroegere machinekamer, waar ooit een heuse stoommachine stond. Deze imposante ruimte van vijf meter hoog heeft een prachtige lichtinval door hoog geplaatste vensters. De zithoek met haard kan volledig worden afgesloten door middel van hoge gordijnen die een kamerscherm vormen. Deze gordijnen zorgen voor extra intimiteit en een betere akoestiek. Keuken, eethoek en zithoek vormen één geheel. Om de band tussen alle ruimtes te versterken, liet Patrick Six alle wanden zwart schilderen, een tint die hij bijzonder goed vindt passen in een industriële context. Hij vindt ook dat je een loft nooit te grondig mag verbouwen, anders wordt het een gewone flat. Daarbij spelen zelfs de materialen een rol. Hier hield hij zich aan de typische industriële materialen als ijzer, glas, beton en baksteen. Het hedendaags karakter komt ook tot uiting door de aankleding met authentiek vintage meubilair.

LE LOFT D'USINE

La région frontalière entre le nord de la France et la Belgique est parsemée d'anciennes usines de textile des xixe et xxe siècles. À Courtrai, on entre dans une ancienne filature où l'architecte Patrick Six a installé son loft et son atelier d'architecture. S'il a à peine touché à l'édifice, il a néanmoins fait peindre l'extérieur en noir. Et sans aucun doute, le caractère fermé de l'extérieur renforce ainsi l'intimité de l'intérieur. Avec son bureau 'Ensemble-1', Six s'est attaqué plus d'une fois à d'anciens bâtiments industriels. Il aime d'ailleurs bien se servir comme point de départ de structures existantes et tant soit peu inhabituelles. Par-ci par-là, une paroi a été percée pour intégrer une fenêtre supplémentaire. Le grand séjour se situe dans l'ancienne salle des machines qui a abrité à l'époque une vraie machine à vapeur. Il y a dans cet espace impressionnant de cinq mètres de haut un très bel éclairage provenant des hautes fenêtres. Le coin salon avec cheminée peut être complètement isolé à l'aide de très hauts rideaux qui forment paravent et confèrent davantage d'intimité et une meilleure acoustique. La cuisine, le coin salle à manger et le coin salon constituent un seul ensemble. Afin de renforcer le lien entre les différents espaces, Patrick Six a fait peindre toutes les parois en noir, une couleur qui, à ses yeux, convient parfaitement au contexte industriel. Il estime aussi qu'il ne faut jamais transformer trop profondément un loft qui risque de devenir sinon un appartement ordinaire. Même les matériaux participent à cette idée. Aussi a-t-il maintenu ici les matériaux typiquement industriels que sont le fer, le verre, le béton et la brique. Mais le côté contemporain se manifeste aussi par la décoration avec d'authentiques meubles vintage.

THE FACTORY LOFT

The border between northern France and Belgium is littered with old 19th and 20th century textile mills. In Kortrijk we step inside an old spinning mill where architect Patrick Six has placed his loft and his architecture studio. He has barely touched the building, but has clad the exterior in a black jacket. The complex looks closed from the outside, enhancing the intimacy of the interior. With his 'Ensemble-1' practice, Six works on converting old industrial buildings. When possible, he likes to start with an existing and somewhat unusual structure. Here and there a wall is broken through to fit an extra window. The large living room is situated in the former engine room where a real steam engine once stood. This impressive five metre high room has wonderful light streaming in through high-up windows. The sitting area with fireplace can be completely screened off with high curtains, providing additional intimacy and better acoustics. Kitchen, dining and sitting area form a single whole. To strengthen the links between the different areas, Patrick Six had all the walls painted black, a colour that for him fits particularly well into an industrial context. He believes you should never over-transform a loft, otherwise it turns into an ordinary apartment. Here the materials themselves play a role. Patrick has kept to typical industrial materials like iron, glass, concrete and brick. The contemporary character is also reflected in the decoration with authentic vintage furniture.

In de vijf meter hoge machinekamer, waarin ooit een heuse stoommachine stond, bracht architect Patrick Six de woonruimte onder. Daar is de zithoek de blikvanger. Omwille van de intimiteit heeft hij rond de zithoek een scherm van gordijnen opgehangen. Deze kunnen in een handomdraai worden geopend.

L'architecte Patrick Six a installé le séjour dans l'ancienne salle des machines qui, avec ses cinq mètres de hauteur, a abrité jadis une authentique machine à vapeur. Les regards s'y portent spontanément sur le coin salon dont l'intimité est protégée par un écran de rideaux qu'il est cependant possible d'ouvrir en un tournemain.

Architect Patrick Six placed the living room in the five metre high engine room, where a real steam engine once stood. The seating corner is the eye catcher here. To give a sense of intimacy he has hung a screen of curtains around the sitting area, which can be opened in a jiffy.

Geniet van het zicht vanuit de zithoek met haard. Eenmaal gesloten zorgen de gordijnen voor het ontstaan van een aparte kamer. Achter de haard vinden we de eethoek en de open keuken. De vele zwarte accenten en wanden zorgen voor de eenheid van architectuur en decoratie.

Admirons cette vue à partir du coin salon avec cheminée. Il suffit de tirer les rideaux pour créer une pièce séparée. Derrière la cheminée se situent le coin salle à manger et la cuisine américaine. Les nombreuses touches et parois noires constituent l'unité de cette architecture et de sa décoration.

Enjoy the view from the sitting area with fireplace. Once closed the curtains create a separate room. Behind the fireplace we find the dining area and the open kitchen. The many black accents and walls give a unity to the architecture and the decoration.

CITYFLAT

COMPACT

Wie plaats zat heeft, kan grenzeloos experimenteren met zijn living room. Dat is natuurlijk een luxe, maar eigenlijk kan dat ook met een beperkte ruimte. Veel hedendaagse stadsappartementen hebben zo'n originele indeling en aankleding. Een stijlvolle bewoning van een krap bemeten ruimte is steeds boeiend om te zien en een voorbeeld voor wie zelf een dergelijke ruimte wil inrichten. Deze flat in het historische hart van Gent omvat ongeveer een verdieping van een herenhuis uit de late negentiende eeuw. De gevel bleef bewaard, maar het interieur werd deels gestript, hoewel een aantal deuren bleef staan. 'Vooral de oude proporties bleven gespaard, waardoor het plafond hoog is', legt bewoonster Lizbeth Nowé uit. Ze is juriste van vorming en werkt in de modesector. Ze ontwerpt niet zelf, maar weet zich omringd door dynamische lui die haar een creatieve boost geven. Ze had een grootvader die beeldhouwer was en een andere die kunst verzamelde. Het grote schilderij van Lucebert komt uit zijn Cobra-collectie. Lizbeth houdt van een echte stadsflat met een compacte keuken. Ze komt ook graag in Amsterdam, waar haar vooral de zwart-witcontrasten in de architectuur opvallen. Die herhaalde ze dan ook in deze ruimte. Liz houdt ook van de combinatie van gladde, strakke elementen met bijvoorbeeld een ruwe houten tafel. Geen van haar spullen komt rechtstreeks uit de winkel, elk object heeft een verhaal en is een trouvaille. 'Een interieur moet immers groeien in de loop van de jaren. Hier ziet alles er vrij hedendaags uit, maar er zit toch weinig nieuws tussen', aldus Lizbeth Nowé.

COMPACT

À condition de disposer d'espace, les possibilités d'expérimenter avec un séjour sont innombrables. Ce qui est évidemment un luxe. Mais un luxe qu'on peut même s'accorder dans un espace restreint. De nombreux appartements contemporains en ville font preuve d'une répartition et d'une décoration originales. L'aménagement stylé d'un espace exigu est toujours passionnant à découvrir, ne fût-ce que parce qu'il donne des idées pour aménager soi-même un tel genre d'espace. Cet appartement dans le centre historique de Gand couvre à peu près un étage d'une maison de maître de la fin du XIXᵉ siècle. Si la façade a été conservée, l'intérieur a été quasiment dénudé à l'exception de quelques portes. « Mais on a surtout sauvegardé les anciennes proportions, notamment la hauteur des plafonds', explique Lizbeth Nowé qui habite là. Juriste de formation, elle travaille dans le secteur de la mode. Elle ne s'adonne pas elle-même au design, mais elle se sait entourée de gens dynamiques qui lui procurent un élan créatif. Elle avait un grand-père sculpteur et un autre collectionneur d'art. Le grand tableau de Lucebert vient d'ailleurs de sa collection Cobra. Lizbeth aime bien ce type de véritable appartement de ville avec sa cuisine compacte. Elle adore aussi se rendre à Amsterdam où elle se laisse impressionner par les contrastes noir et blanc dans l'architecture qu'elle reprend volontiers dans cet espace. Et puis, elle aime aussi la combinaison d'éléments lisses et sobres avec, par exemple, une table de bois brut. Aucune de ses affaires ne provient directement du magasin, chaque objet est une trouvaille avec sa propre histoire. « Il faut qu'un intérieur se développe au fil des ans. Ici, tout a l'air relativement contemporain, mais il y a très peu de neuf », explique Lizbeth Nowé.

COMPACT

People with lots of space can experiment endlessly with their living rooms. This is of course a luxury. But actually you can do so just as well with only limited space. Many contemporary city apartments are laid out and decorated in just such an original way. The way people live in style in a cramped area is always exciting to see and an example for those needing to furnish a similar space. This apartment in the historical heart of Ghent consists of more or less one floor of a late 19th century 'herenhuis' or mansion. The façade was preserved, but the interior was partially stripped, though keeping a number of doors. "But most importantly, the original proportions have been retained, with the high ceilings", explains resident Lizbeth Nowé. Lizbeth is a lawyer by training and works in the fashion industry. She does not design herself, but is surrounded by dynamic people who give her a a creative boost. One grandfather was a sculptor and the other collected art. The large painting by Lucebert comes from his Cobra collection. Lizbeth loves real city flats with small, compact kitchens. She also enjoys travelling to Amsterdam, where she is struck by the black and white contrasts in the architecture, which she also repeats in this room. She also loves to combine smooth, sleek elements with, for example, a rough wooden table. None of her bits and pieces have come directly from a shop, each object is a real find, each with its own story. "An interior has to grow over the years. Everything you can see here looks quite contemporary, but in fact there is little that is new", Lizbeth Nowé says.

De woonkamer is stijlvol en gezellig, met aan de wand een prachtig rek van de Deen Poul Cadovius en aan de muur een doek van Lucebert. De meeste vintage komt uit de collectie van vintageantiquair Hans Soete. Lizbeth houdt van de combinatie van strakke, gladde meubels met ruwe elementen, zoals de houten eettafel, waarrond oude Le Corbusier-stoelen staan.

Le séjour respire simultanément la classe et la convivialité avec sa superbe étagère du Danois Poul Cadovius au mur et une toile de Lucebert. La majeure partie du vintage est issue de la collection de l'antiquaire en vintage Hans Soete. Lizbeth affectionne la combinaison de meubles sobres et lisses avec des éléments plus bruts comme la table à manger en bois entourée de vieilles chaises du Corbusier.

The living room is elegant and friendly, with on the wall a beautiful set of shelves by Dane Poul Cadovius and on the wall a painting by Lucebert. Most of the vintage comes from the collection of vintage dealer Hans Soete. Lizbeth loves the combination of sleek, smooth furniture with rough elements, such as the wooden dining table around which old Corbusier chairs stand.

Lizbeth houdt van frisse zwart-wit-contrasten en koos voor een zwarte keuken en badkamer waarvan de wanden afgewerkt zijn met tadelakt. Maar in de woonkamer is alles helder en transparant, zelfs de vloer is er wit.

Lizbeth aime bien les contrastes noir et blanc et a choisi une cuisine et une salle de bain noires dont les murs ont une finition en tadelakt. Mais dans le séjour, tout est lumineux et transparent, même le sol y est blanc.

Lizbeth likes fresh black and white contrasts and opted for a black kitchen and bathroom with walls finished in tadelakt. But in the living room everything is clear and transparent, even the floor is white.

NEW YORK

ARTISTIEKE LOFT

Deze loft mag dan wel in een drukke wijk van Brussel liggen, binnen merk je daar niets van. We bevinden ons immers in een oude hoedenfabriek achter de straatgevels. Hier woont Dimitri Jeurissen, een van de oprichters van Base Design, samen met zijn artistieke vrouw Jeanna Criscitiello en hun drie kinderen. Toen ze de loft verwierven, woonden ze nog in New York. Ze wonen op de bovenste verdieping en genieten van een riant uitzicht. Door de talrijke vensters baadt de leefruimte in het licht. De loft werd ingedeeld en deels aangekleed door architect Pierre Lhoas. De zuidkant werd helemaal vrij gelaten voor een immense woonruimte met een door Pierre ontworpen bibliotheek, een zithoek, eethoek, open keuken en muziekhoek. Als singer-songwriter bespeelt Jeanna vaak de piano. De bewoners verzamelen al hedendaagse kunst van toen ze in New York woonden. Dimitri komt daar trouwens veel, want Base heeft ook kantoren in New York, Santiago, Barcelona en Madrid. De loft weerspiegelt hun non-conformistische en internationaal gerichte levenswijze. Zelfs de gele keukenkast van Lhoas past daarbij. Het is tevens een zitmeubel en een podium voor de kinderen: hoogst origineel! Jeanna runt samen met enkele collega's in een naburig pand trouwens een succesvol kookatelier. De keuken neemt dus een centrale plaats in. Deze loft lijkt wel een dorp op zich, met een organisch gegroeide structuur, voorzien van straten en pleinen.

UN LOFT ARTISTIQUE

Situé dans un quartier animé de Bruxelles, on s'aperçoit à peine de l'agitation une fois la porte franchie. C'est qu'on se trouve dans une ancienne chapellerie derrière les maisons d'habitation dans la rue. C'est ici que vit Dimitri Jeurissen, un des fondateurs de Base Design, avec sa femme artiste Jeanna Criscitiello et leurs trois enfants. Ayant acquis ce loft alors qu'ils habitaient encore New York, ils occupent l'étage supérieur avec une vue très agréable. Les nombreuses fenêtres inondent d'ailleurs cet espace de vie de lumière. Le loft a été aménagé et partiellement décoré par Pierre Lhoas. Le côté sud a été laissé entièrement libre pour un immense espace de vie avec bibliothèque (créée par Pierre), coin salon, coin salle à manger, cuisine américaine et coin musique. C'est Jeanna en tant que compositeur interprète qui se sert du piano. Les habitants collectionnaient déjà de l'art contemporain lors de leur période newyorkaise. Dimitri y retourne d'ailleurs souvent, car Base a également des bureaux à New York tout comme à Santiago, Barcelone et Madrid. Ce loft reflète tout à fait leur style de vie non conformiste et leur orientation internationale. Même l'armoire de cuisine jaune de Pierre Lhoas s'y intègre bien, qui est en même temps siège et scène pour les enfants. C'est très original ! Avec quelques collègues, Jeanna anime aussi un atelier de cuisine très suivi dans une maison des environs. Il n'est donc pas étonnant que la cuisine occupe une place centrale. En fait, ce loft a un peu l'air d'un village en soi, d'une structure née de manière organique et pourvue de rues et de petites places.

ARTISTIC LOFT

Once inside this loft, you would never know that you are in a busy district of Brussels. We are in a millinery workshop set back from the houses on the street. Here lives Dimitri Jeurissen, one of the founders of Base Design, together with his artist wife Jeanna Criscitiello and their three children. They acquired the loft when they were still living in New York. They live on the top floor and enjoy a splendid view. The many windows bathe the room in light. The loft was partitioned into rooms and partly decorated by architect Pierre Lhoas. The south side was left completely free for an immense living room with wall-to-ceiling bookcase, designed by Pierre, sitting area, dining area, open kitchen and music corner. Jeanna uses the piano as a singer-songwriter. The residents collect contemporary art, as they already did when living in New York. Dimitri travels there a lot, as Base also has offices in New York, Santiago, Barcelona and Madrid. The loft reflects their non-conformist and internationally oriented lifestyle. Even Lhoas's yellow kitchen cupboard fits in, acting very originally as both seating and a stage for the children! With Jeanna also running a successful cookery workshop with some colleagues in a nearby building, the kitchen occupies a central place. This loft is a village in itself, with an organically grown structure of streets and squares.

We vinden deze loft op de hoogste verdieping van een vroegere hoedenfabriek. Architect Pierre Lhoas koos ervoor om de ruimte bijna volledig vrij te laten, waardoor er een immense leefruimte ontstaat met aan de noordzijde de open keuken en daarnaast verschillende zit- en eethoeken, alsook een muziekhoek.

Ce loft est aménagé au dernier étage d'une ancienne chapellerie. L'architecte Pierre Lhoas a choisi de laisser l'espace quasiment entièrement libre, créant ainsi un immense séjour avec, côté nord, la cuisine américaine flanquée de divers coins salons ou salle à manger et même d'un coin musique.

We find this loft on the top floor of a former millinery workshop. Architect Pierre Lhoas has opted to leave the space almost completely free, producing an immense living space with, on the north side, the kitchen and next to it various sitting and dining areas, and a music corner.

Lhoas tekende ook het gele keukenmeubel en de bibliotheekkast, die vol kunstwerken zit. De bewoners woonden lange tijd in New York en begonnen daar een kunstcollectie die blijft aangroeien. Het is een creatieve en artistieke familie die graag vrienden ontvangt. De riante loft straalt gastvrijheid uit.

Lhoas a également dessiné le meuble de cuisine jaune ainsi que la bibliothèque débordante d'œuvres d'art. Les habitants ont longtemps habité New York où ils avaient commencé leur collection d'œuvres d'art qui ne cesse de s'agrandir. La famille aussi artistique que créative adore recevoir des amis et leur loft très agréable respire en effet l'hospitalité.

Lhoas also designed the yellow kitchen element and the built-in bookcase full of artwork. The occupants lived for many years in New York, where they started an art collection that continues to grow. It is a creative and artistic family that loves to receive friends. The spacious loft exudes hospitality.

STYLISH

VINTAGE VILLA

Het Zoute is zowat de meest exquise plek aan de Belgische kust, met witte villa's in het groen. De oude villa's hebben een rustieke stijl en niet zelden een rieten dak. Dat is ook het geval met dit huis, dat een ware gedaanteverwisseling onderging. Het werd vroeger verbouwd door interieurarchitect Lionel Jadot, die er de aankleding uitgooide en de gevels zwart schilderde. De landelijke woning kreeg een hedendaagse look. De keuken en living werden een grote woonruimte met ruwe muren, net een loft. Jadot, die ook films regisseert, houdt van dergelijke filmdecors. Ondertussen woont hier Bea Mombaers, tot ver over de grenzen bekend als decorateur. Ze richtte tal van woningen in die worden gepubliceerd door de internationale vakpers. Haar inbreng is net zo boeiend, omdat ze van de living room een bijzondere plek maakte. Door het kiezen voor uitgelezen stukken vintage design en kunst uit de jaren zeventig en tachtig, creëert ze een contemporaine woning met een artistieke uitstraling. En dat past perfect bij Het Zoute, waar altijd al veel kunstenaars rondhangen of exposeren in de talrijke gerenommeerde galeries. Het is boeiend om te zien dat het culturele leven van de hele streek zo zijn weerspiegeling vindt. Ze combineert moeiteloos oud en nieuw, gaaf en ruw, met onder meer meubelen van Jules Wabbes, Willy Van Der Meeren, Harry Bertoia, Joe Colombo en witte reliëfs van Gilbert Swimberghe. Ze is persoonlijk tuk op design van beeldende kunstenaars of architecten die, volgens haar, de vormgeving een extra dimensie schenken.

VINTAGE VILLAS

Het Zoute is is probably the most exquisite place on the Belgian coast, with its white villas set in the green countryside. The old villas are rustic in style, many of them with thatched roofs – including this house that underwent a metamorphosis. It had already been converted by interior architect Lionel Jadot, who threw out the decorations and painted the walls black. The rural home was given a contemporary look. The kitchen and living room became a single large living room with rough walls, like a loft. Jadot, who also directs films, loves this sort of film set. Today the house is home to Bea Mombaers, an interior decorator known well beyond Belgium. She has designed many homes featured in the international press. Her contribution is equally fascinating in the way she has made the living room into a special space. Using exquisite pieces of vintage '70s and '80s design and art, she creates a contemporary home with an artistic feel to it. Which fits perfectly with Het Zoute, where many artists have homes or exhibit in numerous prestigious galleries. It is fascinating to see such a reflection of the cultural life of the entire region. Mombaers effortlessly combines old and new, cool and rough, including furniture by Jules Wabbes, Willy Van Der Meeren, Harry Bertoia, Joe Colombo and white reliefs by Gilbert Swimberghe. She is personally keen on visual artists or architects who, for her, give design an additional dimension.

VINTAGE VILLA

Avec ses villas blanches dans la verdure, Le Zoute est sans doute l'endroit le plus exquis de toute la côte belge. Les anciennes villas arborent un style rustique et les toits de chaume n'y sont pas rares. C'est notamment le cas de cette maison qui a subi une véritable métamorphose lorsqu'elle a d'abord été transformée par l'architecte d'intérieur Lionel Jadot. S'étant débarrassé de la décoration, il en fit peindre les murs en noir, conférant à cette demeure rustique un look contemporain. Il réunit la cuisine et le séjour en un seul grand espace aux murs bruts, style loft. Comme il était également réalisateur de cinéma, Jadot affectionnait ce genre de décors de films. La maison est habitée actuellement par Bea Mombaers, une décoratrice de renommée internationale. Bon nombre de ses réalisations se retrouvent publiées dans la presse professionnelle internationale. Sa contribution est spécialement passionnante parce qu'elle a fait du séjour un endroit particulier. En sélectionnant des pièces choisies de design et d'art vintage des années soixante-dix et quatre-vingts, elle a créé une demeure contemporaine au rayonnement artistique, tout à fait dans l'ambiance du Zoute, depuis toujours un lieu fréquenté par des artistes qui exposent souvent dans les nombreuses galeries renommées. Il est passionnant de voir comment la vie culturelle de toute la région s'y reflète. Elle combine sans le moindre problème l'ancien et le neuf, le brut et le raffiné avec, parmi d'autres, du mobilier de Jules Wabbes, Willy Van Der Meeren, Harry Bertoia, Joe Colombo et des reliefs blancs de Gilbert Swimberghe. Personnellement, elle affectionne le design d'artistes plasticiens ou d'architectes qui procurent à ses yeux une dimension supplémentaire au stylisme.

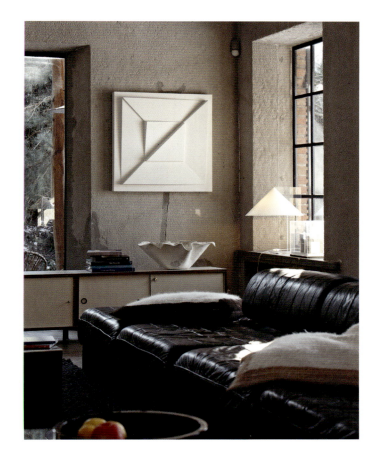

Het rustieke interieur van de villa ruimde plaats voor een enorme woonruimte, net een loft, waarvan de leefruimte en kookhoek in elkaar lopen. De muren zijn ruw gecementeerd. Deze grijze wanden en de betonnen vloer zorgen voor een mooi contrast met het designmeubilair.

L'intérieur rustique de la villa a cédé la place a un immense séjour, presque comme un loft, sans distinction nette entre le coin cuisine et l'espace de vie. Les murs sont recouverts de ciment brut et ces parois grises avec le sol en béton contrastent joliment avec le mobilier design.

The villa's rustic interior made way for a huge living space, like a loft, with the living room and kitchenette running into each other. The rough cement grey walls and the concrete floor contrast attractively with the designer furniture.

Bea Mombaers heeft oog voor actuele trends. Ze richt heel wat huizen in met vintage en hedendaagse ontwerpen. Ze houdt ook van sculpturale objecten, die ze overal in haar interieur laat slingeren. Haar interieurs zijn altijd heerlijk nonchalant van stijl.

Bea Mombaers a certes l'œil pour les tendances contemporaines. Elle aménage des tas de maisons avec du vintage et quelques objets contemporains. Elle aime aussi les objets sculpturaux qu'elle laisse traîner un peu partout chez elle. Aussi ses intérieurs sont toujours d'un style nonchalant.

Bea Mombaers has an eye for current trends. She decorates lots of houses with vintage and more contemporary designs. She also loves sculptured *objets* that lie around everywhere in her interior. Her interiors are always nonchalant.

ART COLLECTOR

SEVENTIES-CHARME

Velen kijken neer op flats uit de jaren zeventig. We geven toe dat sommige appartementen uit die tijd buitengewoon saai zijn, maar je had architecten die toch iets origineels bedachten. De flat van de Brusselse vintageantiquair Jean-Claude Jacquemart is in ieder geval een eyecatcher. Deze plek zag er voor de komst van Jean-Claude wel burgerlijk uit, met een simpel houten trapje en een minder strenge vormgeving. Hij voegde daar een portie Bauhausstijl aan toe en creëerde een strakke witte trap met een constructivistisch balkon voor een mezzanine. Jean-Claude verhuist vaak en telkens maakt hij een nieuwe selectie van zijn collectie. Het is trouwens een uiteenlopende verzameling met oudheden, veel kunst en objecten uit de twintigste eeuw. Hij is gek op boeken en lampen, zoals zijn lampen van René Mathieu en Angelo Lelli. Hij is ook helemaal weg van de jaren vijftig, maar is geen designfreak die louter grote namen zoekt. Anonieme ontwerpen vindt hij net zo boeiend. Zijn stijl is vrij eclectisch. Naast een werk van Bram Bogart hangt hij een zeventiende-eeuws tableau. Hij wil dus geen living met één stijl, maar er moet wel een rode draad in de collectie schuilen. Denk nu niet dat hij zich een echte designfanaat voelt. Hij houdt zelfs niet van designhotels die op woningen lijken. Voor Jean-Claude is niet de stijl van een interieur, maar wel de persoonlijkheid van belang. En in een woning moet je nog iets kunnen ontdekken, zelfs als bewoner.

LE CHARME DES SEVENTIES

Beaucoup considèrent les appartements des années 1970 avec dédain et il faut admettre que certains de cette époque sont extrêmement ennuyeux. Il y a eu cependant quelques architectes pour concevoir des choses originales. Ainsi, l'appartement de l'antiquaire de vintage bruxellois Jean-Claude Jacquemart ne peut manquer d'attirer les regards. Avec un simple escalier en bois et des lignes pas trop sévères, il avait l'air très bourgeois avant l'arrivée de Jean-Claude. Mais ce dernier y ajouta une bonne portion de style Bauhaus et créa notamment un escalier blanc très sobre avec un balcon constructiviste pour une mezzanine. Comme Jean-Claude déménage souvent, il sélectionne à chaque fois de nouveaux objets de sa collection très diversifiée d'antiquités et de nombreux objets d'art et des pièces du xxe siècle. Il raffole entre autres de livres et de lampes, surtout des lampes de René Mathieu et d'Angelo Lelli. Tout comme il adore aussi les années 1950, sans toutefois idolâtrer uniquement les grands noms de cette époque car il peut se passionner tout autant pour des objets anonymes. Dans son style plutôt éclectique, il accroche volontiers une œuvre de Bram Bogart à côté d'un tableau du dix-septième. S'il ne veut donc pas de style unique pour son séjour, il observe néanmoins un fil rouge pour sa collection. Mais il n'est certes pas un fanatique du design, il abhorre même les hôtels design qui ressemblent à des habitations. Ce qui compte aux yeux de Jean-Claude, ce n'est pas le style d'un intérieur mais la personnalité. Et il faut toujours pouvoir découvrir quelque chose dans une maison, même quand on y habite.

SEVENTIES CHARM

Many people scoff at '70s flats. Admittedly many apartments from that decade are extraordinarily dull. But there were also architects who knew how to come up with something original. Brussels vintage antique dealer Jean-Claude Jacquemart's flat is certainly an eye catcher. Before Jean-Claude's arrival, this place looked pretty bourgeois, with a simple wooden staircase and a less rigorous design. To it he added a serving of Bauhaus, creating a sleek white staircase with a constructivist balcony-mezzanine. Jean-Claude moves home often and each time makes a new selection from his collection. This is a diverse collection of antiques, with much 20th century art and objects. He is crazy about books and lamps, like those of René Mathieu and Angelo Lelli. While he also loves the '50s, he is not a design freak who goes only for the big names. Anonymous designs he finds just as exciting. His style is quite eclectic. A seventeenth century painting hangs next to a work by Bram Bogart. He does not want a one-style living room, though there has to be a common denominator somewhere in the collection. Don't think that he sees himself as a design fanatic. He has no love for design hotels that resemble houses. For Jean-Claude it is not the style of an interior, but the personality that counts. You need to be able to still discover things in a house, even when it's your own home.

Voor de komst van Jean-Claude Jacquemart was dit een kleinburgerlijke flat uit de jaren zeventig, met een schriele trap en houten deuren. Jean-Claude is tuk op Bauhaus-architectuur en liet daarom de trap en mezzanine opnieuw kneden alsof het betonarchitectuur was, maar dit is het niet. Deze forse witte volumes zijn een ideale context voor zijn decoratie met veel Italiaanse vintage lampen en wat moderne kunst.

Avant l'arrivée de Jean-Claude Jacquemart, ceci était un appartement petit-bourgeois des années '70 avec un maigre escalier et des portes en bois. Adorant le style architectural Bauhaus, Jean-Claude a fait remodeler l'escalier et la mezzanine comme s'il s'agissait d'une architecture en béton, ce qu'ils ne sont évidemment pas. Mais ces puissants volumes blancs forment le contexte idéal pour sa décoration avec un bon nombre de lampes vintage italien et un peu d'art moderne.

Before Jean-Claude Jacquemart's arrival this was a bourgeois apartment from the '70s, with a gaunt staircase and wooden doors. Jean-Claude is keen on Bauhaus architecture and had the staircase and mezzanine remoulded as if it were concrete architecture, though it is not. These harsh white volumes are an ideal context for decorating with lots of Italian vintage lamps and some modern art.

131

Jean-Claude verhuist om de twee à drie jaar. Telkens koopt hij nieuwe objecten, maar kiest hij ook stukken uit zijn collectie. Het is trouwens een uiteenlopende verzameling, van vooral twintigste-eeuwse kunst, maar hier en daar ook een ouder stuk. Hij houdt van kleine schilderijen, tekeningen en prenten om volledige wanden mee te bekleden.

Jean-Claude déménage tous les deux ou trois ans et s'entoure à chaque fois de nouveaux objets, tout en puisant aussi dans sa propre collection, un ensemble disparate d'objets d'art essentiellement du XXe siècle, avec par-ci par-là quelques pièces plus anciennes. Il aime bien les petits tableaux, dessins ou images pour en recouvrir des murs entiers.

Jean-Claude moves house every two or three years. And every time he buys new objects, but also selects from his collection. It is a very diverse collection, mostly of 20th century art, but with an older piece here and there. He loves covering walls completely with small paintings, drawings and prints.

132

FIFTIES & CONTEMPO-RARY

Dit is geen grote flat, maar door de klare aankleding en het vele licht merk je dat niet. Er is
zelfs plaats voor een haardvuur. Bewoner Tim
Dubus houdt van een spontane decoratie en
van sculpturale objecten, zoals de wandrekjes
van Il Laboratorio dell'imperfetto.

Si cet appartement n'est pas grand, on s'en
aperçoit à peine parce qu'il laisse entrer
beaucoup de lumière et que sa décoration
est bien claire. Son occupant, Tim Dubus,
aime la décoration spontanée et les objets
sculpturaux comme ces étagères de 'Il
Laboratorio dell'Imperfetto'.

This is not a large apartment, but with the
light-coloured furnishing and lots of light
you wouldn't know. There is even room for
an open fireplace. Occupant Tim Dubus
loves both spontaneous decoration and
sculptural objects, such as the shelving from
'Il Laboratorio dell'imperfetto'.

PURE

PROUVÉ

Een paar prachtige buitenzichten verraden meteen dat deze woning op het platteland ligt. Vanuit de riante woonruimte met een lange eettafel krijg je een uitzicht over het polderlandschap, waar in de verte de middeleeuwse toren van Lissewege opdoemt. Het contrast van de omgeving met de woning is groot, want het interieur heeft zelfs wat grootstedelijke allure. Het strak uitgelijnde interieur met een duidelijk rasterpatroon laat heel wat leefruimte toe. Onlangs liet de bewoner een extra verdieping op zijn woning bouwen. Hiervoor werkte Hans Soete samen met architect Pascal Van Der Kelen en interieurvormgever Frederic Hooft, die net als hij tuk is op vintage design. Hans' passie voor design begon bij het inrichten van deze woning. Zo ontdekte hij onder meer het design uit de jaren vijftig. Zijn dierbaarste vondst is het rode militaire bureau van Jean Prouvé dat in de woonruimte boven ophangt aan de muur. Dit is ook zijn geliefkoosde werkplek. Frederic Hooft gaf eveneens de sauna vorm. Deze werd helemaal bekleed met polyester en voorzien van blauwe deuren die net een kamerscherm vormen. Hans vindt in deze woning wel wat van zijn passie voor architectuur terug. Hij houdt van vrij transparante ruimtes die verre doorzichten toelaten en een ideaal kader vormen voor zijn vintage design, dat hij op deze manier van alle kanten kan bewonderen. Hij houdt van stoelen, zetels en lampen die meer op sculpturen dan op meubels lijken.

PROUVÉ

Il suffit de s'arrêter un instant aux superbes paysages pour se rendre compte que cette habitation est située à la campagne. À partir de l'agréable séjour avec sa longue table à manger, on a une belle vue sur les polders où s'élève au loin la tour médiévale de Lissewege. Mais l'allure de la maison a quelque chose de la grande ville et forme donc un grand contraste avec les environs. Les lignes sobres de l'intérieur et le modèle évident de trame créent de beaux espaces de vie. En plus, l'occupant vient d'ajouter un étage supplémentaire à la maison. Hans Soete a fait appel pour cela à l'architecte Pascal Van Der Kelen et au styliste d'intérieur Frederic Hooft, tout comme lui un passionné de design vintage. Cette passion du design s'est manifestée chez Hans quand il a aménagé cette maison. C'est alors qu'il découvrit, entre autres, le design des années cinquante. Sa trouvaille la plus précieuse est le bureau militaire rouge de Jean Prouvé suspendu au mur dans le séjour en haut. C'est aussi son lieu de travail préféré. Frederic Hooft a également dessiné le sauna couvert entièrement de polyester et pourvu de portes bleues qui suggèrent un paravent. Dans cette maison, Hans retrouve en grande partie sa passion pour l'architecture. Il aime les espaces transparents qui laissent passer le regard et forment le cadre idéal pour sa collection de vintage qu'il peut admirer ainsi de tous les côtés. Pour lui, les chaises, fauteuils et lampes peuvent très bien ressembler davantage à des sculptures qu'à des meubles.

PROUVÉ

Beautiful outdoor views immediately tell us we are in the country. From the spacious living room with its long dining table you look out over the polder landscape with the medieval tower of Lissewege looming in the distance. This is in sharp contrast to the house itself, where the interior has a rather big city feel to it. The tightly drawn interior with its clear grid pattern provides plenty of living space. Recently its occupier had an additional floor built on. For this Hans Soete worked with architect Pascal Van Der Kelen and interior designer Frederic Hooft who like him is also a fan of vintage design. Hans's passion for design started when furnishing this house. Which is how he discovered '50s design. His most precious find is the Jean Prouvé red military desk that now hangs on the living room wall. This is also his favourite workplace. Frederic Hooft also designed the sauna entirely covered with polyester and with blue doors forming a screen. The house echoes some of Hans's passion for architecture. He is fond of open, transparent spaces offering distant vistas, forming an ideal framework for his vintage design that he can admire from all sides. He loves chairs, sofas and lamps that look more like sculptures than furniture.

Deze villa heeft een simpel maar handig grondplan. Aan de zuidzijde is er een grote living room met nogal wat meubels en lampen uit de jaren vijftig. Bewoner Hans Soete werd bij de stoffering van zijn interieur geraakt door het design uit die periode. Ondertussen ging hij ook verzamelen en is nu zelfs vintageantiquair.

Le plan de cette villa est tout simple mais fort pratique. Côté sud, il y a un grand séjour avec pas mal de mobilier et de lampes des années '50. En habillant son intérieur, Hans Soete a été frappé par le design de cette époque. S'étant mis à le collectionner, il est depuis lui-même antiquaire de vintage.

This villa has a simple but practical floor plan. To the south is a large living room with plenty of furniture and lamps from the '50s. It was when furnishing his interior that occupant Hans Soete was struck by the design of this period. He began collecting and today is himself a vintage antique dealer.

Oorspronkelijk was de woning een bungalow waarop Hans achteraf een verdieping bouwde, ingericht door Frederic Hooft. Het gaat om een extra relaxruimte met sauna. Hooft stopte de sauna achter de blauwe deuren van een soort kamerscherm.

À l'origine, cette demeure était un bungalow sur lequel Hans a fait construire plus tard un étage aménagé par Frederic Hooft. Il s'agit d'un espace de détente supplémentaire avec sauna. Hooft a installé ce sauna derrière les portes bleues de ce qui ressemble à un paravent.

This home was originally a bungalow to which Hans later added another floor, arranged by Frederic Hooft, to form an additional relaxation area with sauna. Hooft tucked the sauna away behind the blue doors of a kind of room divider.

ARTISTIC

'Ik verkies eenvoudige oplossingen, hou niet van echte decoratie en vind vooral dat de verhoudingen van ruimtes, lichtinval en materialen moeten kloppen', aldus interieurvormgeefster Élise Van Thuyne. Ze verbouwt liefst een oud pand, omdat dit meteen een verhaal vertelt dat herschreven kan worden. En vooral omdat ze in een bestaand gebouw interessante toevalligheden ontdekt, een deur of een tegelwand waarmee ze weer iets nieuws aanvangt. Élise houdt van de verbanden tussen interieur en exterieur, tussen woning en bewoner, tussen licht en kleur. Ze vindt het fascinerend om een woning te zien verouderen en vindt de samenwerking met ambachtslui heel belangrijk. Ze ontwerpt interieurs trouwens ook deels op de werf. Haar woning is het voormalige boswachtershuis van het kasteel van Ooidonk. Het laat negentiende-eeuwse pandje doet wat denken aan een oud station. Aan het interieur werd amper gesleuteld. Boven de schouw hangt een ijzeren rek om kleren op te hangen, daaronder staat een achterpootloze buiszetel van Bas van Pelt. De tafel werd ontworpen door Jos Devriendt, met wie ze veel samenwerkt. Daarnaast situeert zich de zithoek in een apart kamertje. De kleine keuken verschuilt zich achter de oude haard. Haar atelier in een oud schuurtje is schitterend, met een vloer van keien. Élise Van Thuyne houdt van ruwe en robuuste materialen, niet burgerlijk en met een artistieke uitstraling. In dit atelier, waar ze het grootste deel van haar tijd doorbrengt, put ze inspiratie uit het zicht op de velden.

UN BIOTOPE ARTISTIQUE

« J'ai une préférence pour les solutions simples, je n'aime pas trop la décoration et j'estime surtout qu'il faut veiller aux bons rapports entre les espaces, la lumière et les matériaux. » Ainsi parle la styliste d'intérieur Élise Van Thuyne. Elle aime surtout réhabiliter d'anciennes demeures parce qu'elles racontent une histoire qu'elle peut ensuite réécrire. Et surtout parce qu'elle découvre dans un bâtiment existant des éléments fortuits intéressants, comme par exemple une porte ou un mur carrelé dont elle peut se servir pour faire du neuf. Élise aime les rapports entre intérieur et extérieur, entre une maison et son occupant, entre la lumière et les couleurs. Elle trouve fascinant de voir vieillir une maison et accorde une grande importance à la collaboration avec les artisans. Elle conçoit d'ailleurs partiellement ses intérieurs sur le chantier même. Sa propre maison est l'ancienne maison du garde forestier du château d'Ooidonk, petite propriété datant du XIXᵉ siècle qui évoque un peu une ancienne gare et dont elle a laissé l'intérieur quasiment intact. Au-dessus de la cheminée est suspendu un séchoir en fer pour accrocher les vêtements, en dessous se trouve un fauteuil en tuyaux sans pied arrière de Bas van Pelt. La table a été dessinée par Jos Devriendt avec qui elle collabore souvent. À côté, dans une petite pièce séparée, se situe le coin salon. La petite cuisine se cache derrière l'âtre ancien. Avec son revêtement de sol en cailloux, son atelier dans une vieille petite grange est simplement superbe. Élise Van Thuyne aime en effet les matériaux bruts et robustes, pas bourgeois pour un sou et qui dégagent un air artistique. C'est dans cet atelier où elle passe le plus clair de son temps, qu'elle puise son inspiration dans la vue des champs.

ARTISTIC BIOTOPE

"I opt for simple solutions. I don't go for decoration in the full sense of the term. It's particularly important for me that the proportions of the rooms, the incoming light and the materials are right", says interior designer Élise Van Thuyne. What she likes best is transforming an old building, because it immediately tells a story that can be rewritten. And in an existing building especially, one discovers interesting coincidences, a door or a tiled wall with which one can start something new. Élise loves the interplay between interior and exterior, between house and occupant, between light and colour. She is fascinated watching a house age. Working also with craftsmen is very important for her. She designs interiors partly on site. Her own home is the former forester's house of Ooidonk castle. This late 19th century building has something of an old station building about it. She has left the interior largely untouched. Above the fireplace hangs an iron clothes rack, and under it a Bas van Pelt cantilever tubular chair. The table was designed by Jos Devriendt, with whom she regularly collaborates. The lounge is situated next to it in a separate little room. The small kitchen is hidden behind the old fireplace. Her studio in an old shed is a marvellous place with a pebble floor. Élise Van Thuyne loves rough and rugged materials, not bourgeois at all and with an artistic feel to them. In this workshop, where she spends most of her time, she draws inspiration from the view over the fields.

De zitkamer vinden we in een aparte uitbouw van de woning, waarvan de authentieke vloer met rode plavuizen is bewaard. Ook de glas-in-loodramen herinneren ons aan de ouderdom van dit boswachtershuis. Hier bouwde Élise een grote bibliotheek en zette daarvoor een prachtige zitbank van Jules Wabbes en rechts een zit van Maarten Van Severen. Op de vorige pagina lopen we even door haar ontwerpatelier.

Le salon dont le sol authentique de carreaux de terre cuite rouges a été conservé, se situe dans un arrière-corps de cette demeure. De même, les fenêtres en vitrail rappellent l'ancienneté de cette maison de garde forestier. C'est ici qu'Élise a installé une grande bibliothèque avec un superbe divan de Jules Wabbes et à droite un siège de Maarten Van Severen. La page précédente nous emmène dans son atelier de création.

The lounge is in a separate outhouse which has retained its original red-tiled floor. The leaded windows too remind us of the age of this forester's cottage. Here Élise built a large bookcase and placed in front of it a beautiful Jules Wabbes sofa and to the right a chair by Maarten Van Severen. On the previous page we walk through her design studio.

STUDIOLO

ZONDER BELLE ÉPOQUE

Deze woning mag dan wel tussen de belle-époquehuizen staan, het pand is een industriële ruimte uit de jaren zestig. Er stond ooit wel een sierlijk herenhuis, dat werd gesloopt voor de bouw van dit voormalig naaiatelier. Nu wordt het betrokken door Wouter Hoste en Harvey Bouterse, die beiden actief zijn als stylist in de modesector. Het bouwwerk werd door architect Kris Mys tot woning verbouwd. Het atelier bevindt zich beneden, en boven wordt er gewoond. Vooral de woonruimte, helemaal boven, met binnenterras, is uniek. Er is zelfs een haardvuur om het helemaal gezellig te maken. De grote glaspartijen zorgen voor licht en transparantie. De afwerking van de ruimtes is sober, met vloeren van gepolijst beton en ruwe wanden die de ateliersfeer kracht bijzetten. Maar een strak interieur is het niet, daarvoor zijn Wouter en Harvey te enthousiaste verzamelaars. Eerst verzamelden ze vintage lampen, maar al snel ontdekten ze de keramiek uit de jaren vijftig en zestig. Ze hebben vooral belangstelling voor het werk van Vlaamse ateliers als Perignem en Amphora. Ondertussen hebben ze een unieke verzameling en maken ze nu ook zelf keramiek. Hun interieur evolueert constant, de stukken verhuizen van kamer naar kamer en er komt snel wat bij. Het is boeiend om te zien hoe mooi mode en kunstambacht hier op een hedendaagse wijze met elkaar versmelten: een contemporaine symbiose.

SANS BELLE ÉPOQUE

Bien que située parmi des maisons Belle époque, cette propriété est un espace industriel datant des années 1960. L'élégante maison de maître qui s'y trouvait avait en effet été remplacée par cet ancien atelier de couture. Aujourd'hui, l'endroit est habité par Wouter Hoste et Harvey Bouterse, tous deux stylistes dans le secteur de la mode. L'édifice a été transformé en habitation par l'architecte Kris Mys. L'atelier est demeuré au rez-de-chaussée, surmonté de la partie habitation. On apprécie surtout l'aspect unique de l'espace de vie tout en haut avec une terrasse intérieure. Il y a même un feu ouvert, touche ultime de convivialité, tandis que les grandes surfaces vitrées donnent une belle lumière et beaucoup de transparence. La finition des espaces est très sobre, avec des sols en béton poli et des parois brutes qui accentuent l'ambiance atelier. Mais ce n'est finalement pas un intérieur sévère parce que Wouter et Harvey sont des collectionneurs débordant d'enthousiasme. Après s'être intéressés pour les lampes vintage, ils ont bien vite découvert la céramique des années 1950 et 1960, surtout celle des ateliers flamands comme Perignem et Amphora. Ils en possèdent depuis une collection unique et se sont, en plus, mis eux-mêmes à la céramique. Leur intérieur évolue constamment, les pièces déménagent d'un endroit à l'autre et il en vient toujours plus. Il est aussi fort passionnant de voir comment la mode et l'artisanat se rejoignent d'une manière tout à fait actuelle : une symbiose contemporaine.

WITHOUT BELLE ÉPOQUE

Despite the surrounding *belle époque* houses, the property is an industrial building from the '60s. The graceful mansion that once stood here was demolished to make way for this former dressmaking workshop. It is now occupied by Wouter Hoste and Harvey Bouterse, who both work as stylists in the fashion industry. The building was converted by architect Kris Mys into a dwelling. The studio is below and the living area above. The living room, right at the top, with an interior patio, is unique. There is even a fireplace to give a cosy feel. The large glass windows provide light and transparency. The finishing of the rooms is austere, with polished concrete floors and rough walls that reinforce the studio atmosphere. But it is not a harsh interior, as both Wouter and Harvey are enthusiastic collectors. First they collected vintage lamps, but soon discovered '50s and '60s ceramics. They are particularly interested in the work of Flemish workshops like Perignem and Amphora. Meanwhile they have a unique collection and now also make their own ceramics. Their interior is constantly evolving, with pieces moving from room to room and constant additions. It is fascinating to see how beautifully fashion and craftsmanship meld here in a contemporary manner to produce a modern-day symbiosis.

Dit gebouw was dus eerder een naaiatelier en nu het woon- en modeatelier van Wouter Hoste (links) en Harvey Bouterse (rechts), die op de vorige pagina staan. Ze zijn tuk op vintage. Hier zie je hun bibliotheek met de twee zetels van de Braziliaan Sergio Rodrigues. Wouter en Harvey verzamelen niet alleen keramiek uit de jaren vijftig en zestig: Wouter is ondertussen ook zelf als keramist actief.

Cet ancien atelier de couture est actuellement la maison et l'atelier de mode de Wouter Hoste (à gauche) et Harvey Bouterse (à droite), qu'on retrouve à la page précédente. Ils adorent le vintage. Voici leur bibliothèque avec deux fauteuils du Brésilien Sergio Rodrigues. Non content de collectionner avec son compère Harvey de la céramique des années '50 et '60, Wouter s'y est mis lui-même et travaille comme céramiste.

This building was once a dressmaking workshop and is now the living and fashion studio of Wouter Hoste (left) and Harvey Bouterse (right), shown on the previous page. They are keen on vintage. Here you see their library with the two chairs by Brazilian Sergio Rodrigues. Wouter and Harvey not only collect '50s and '60s ceramics, Wouter is now also an active ceramist.

Links vang je een glimp op van hun verzameling keramiek en rechts zie je Harvey in zijn ontwerpruimte. In deze woning vloeien de woon- en werkruimtes gewoon in elkaar over.

À gauche, un petit coup d'œil sur la collection de céramique et à droite, Harvey dans son espace de création. Dans cette maison, les espaces de vie et de travail débordent l'un dans l'autre.

To the left you catch a glimpse of their ceramics collection and to the right we see Harvey in his design area. In this house the living and working areas blend into each other.

Helemaal bovenaan het gebouw, op drie hoog, vinden we een grote leefruimte met zithoek en leefkeuken. Rond de tafel staan stoelen van de Nederlandse ontwerper Cees Braakman. Omwille van het licht werd er midden in de ruimte een terras gecreëerd. Van hieruit geniet je ook van een spannend uitzicht op de daken van de stad.

Tout en haut, au troisième étage, se situent un grand séjour avec un coin salon et un séjour cuisine. La table est entourée de chaises du créateur néerlandais Cees Braakman. Afin de capter la lumière, une terrasse a été créée en plein milieu de l'espace. Elle offre en même temps une vue passionnante sur les toits de la ville.

Right at the top of the building, on the third floor, we find a large living room with seating area and kitchen. Around the table are chairs by Dutch designer Cees Braakman. To provide light, a patio was created in the middle of the room. From here we also enjoy an exciting view over the city rooftops.

GREEN

HEDENDAAGSE BOSWONING

Voor sommige ontwerpers is de intimiteit van de architectuur belangrijker dan de monumentaliteit. Interieurarchitect Jean-Denis Sacré ontwierp deze boswoning als een woonkast met laden en deuren. Het is een compacte en ecologische woning vol intimiteit en helemaal op mensenschaal ontworpen. De talrijke doorzichten zorgen voor ruimte. Het is geen volledig nieuwe woonst, Sacré vertrok van een bestaande constructie uit de jaren zeventig. De basisstructuur werd aangevuld met terrassen die in de zomer dienstdoen als woonruimte. Zo breidde hij de eerder kleine woonkamer uit voor het warme seizoen. Zelfs naast de slaapkamer kwam er een terras, afgesloten met houten planken. Door de talrijke deuren en vensters, die al dan niet met luiken kunnen worden afgesloten, kan de woning bijvoorbeeld 's avonds of in de winter gesloten en in de zomer open en transparant zijn. Het licht valt van alle kanten binnen en beweegt extra veel door het bladerdek van de bomen rond het huis. In het bos is het leven met de natuur een waar genot. De binnenstructuur van de woning is compact en lijkt wat op een Japanse kast. Jean-Denis houdt dan ook van kasten en vernuftig bedachte opbergruimtes. Ook doorzichten vindt hij boeiend. Hier kijk je vanuit de woonkamer dwars door het huis. De ontwerper koos voor een zacht getint kleurenpalet. Hij houdt niet van te hard licht en verkiest de natuurlijke teint van eik, natuursteen en keien.

UNE MAISON FORESTIÈRE CONTEMPORAINE

Pour certains créateurs, l'intimité d'une architecture est plus importante que la monumentalité. L'architecte d'intérieur Jean-Denis Sacré a conçu cette maison forestière comme une armoire d'habitation avec des tiroirs et des portes. Il s'agit d'une demeure compacte et écologique marquée par l'intimité et tout à fait à échelle humaine. Les nombreuses percées donnent une sensation d'espace. Ce n'est pas une construction entièrement neuve puisque Sacré est parti d'une maison existante des années 1970. Il a complété la structure de base par des terrasses qui servent d'espace de vie en été, agrandissant ainsi le modeste séjour pour la belle saison. Même la chambre à coucher a été dotée d'une terrasse fermée par des planches. Grâce aux nombreuses portes et fenêtres qu'il est possible ou non de fermer par des volets, la maison peut être bien fermée le soir ou en hiver et très ouverte et transparente en été. Pénétrant de tous les côtés, la lumière est très mouvante par le jeu des feuillages des arbres entourant la maison. C'est un vrai délice de vivre ainsi en contact étroit avec la nature. La structure intérieure de la maison est compacte et ressemble un peu à une armoire japonaise. Jean-Denis aime bien les armoires et les rangements ingénieux. La profondeur du regard le passionne aussi et ici, par exemple, on regarde à partir du séjour à travers toute la maison. Pour les teintes, notre designer a opté pour une palette de couleurs douces. Il n'aime pas trop la lumière crue et préfère les teintes naturelles du chêne, de la pierre de taille et des galets.

CONTEMPORARY FOREST HOME

For some designers, intimacy in architecture is more important than monumentality. Interior designer Jean-Denis Sacré designed this forest home as a 'living cupboard' complete with with drawers and doors. It is a compact, ecological dwelling, full of intimacy and entirely on a human scale. The numerous vistas provide space. It is not a completely new house: Sacré started from an existing structure dating from the '70s. The basic structure was then supplemented with terraces which serve in the summer as living quarters. In this way he expanded the rather small living room for the warm season. Next to the bedroom came a terrace, closed off with wooden planks. The numerous doors and windows, with or without shutters, enable the house to be closed during evenings or winter, and open and transparent in summer. Light comes in from all sides, shifting with the leaves of the trees that surround the house. Living with nature in the forest is a real pleasure. The inner structure of the house is compact and resembles a Japanese cabinet. Jean-Denis loves cupboards and ingeniously contrived storage spaces. He is also fascinated by vistas. Here you look from the living room right through the house. The designer has opted for a softly tinted colour palette. He does not like overly harsh light and prefers the natural tones of oak, natural stone and boulders.

De meeste moderne ontwerpers houden van monumentaliteit. Maar interieurontwerper Jean-Denis Sacré is een uitzondering. Hij zweert bij intimiteit en bouwde een compacte woning die ons een beetje doet denken aan een Japanse kast. Hij creëerde ook lagen tussen interieur en exterieur, zoals de twee binnenterrassen.

Par rapport à la plupart des stylistes modernes qui aiment la monumentalité, Jean-Denis Sacré est une exception. Privilégiant l'intimité pour ses créations d'intérieurs, il a construit une maison compacte avec un petit air d'armoire japonaise. Il a également prévu des strates entre l'intérieur et l'extérieur sous forme de deux terrasses closes.

Most modern designers go for monumentality. But interior designer Jean-Denis Sacré is an exception, he swears by intimacy and built a compact house that is more than a little reminiscent of a Japanese cabinet. He also created layers between the inside and outside, like the two inner patios.

INTIMATE

INTIMATE

Wandelend door dit interieur denk je onvermijdelijk aan de schilderijen van de zeventiende-eeuwse Hollandse meester Pieter de Hooch, die prachtige interieurs schilderde met een vertederend licht. Datzelfde licht sijpelt ook dit huis binnen. Aan de straatzijde heeft het bijna volledig blinde gevels, maar het opent zich aan de tuinzijde. Maar niet zoals een hedendaagse woning met grote vensters die het exterieur gewoon helemaal binnenlaten. Hier wordt de grens tussen binnen en buiten stijlvol gedoseerd door hoge ramen en kleine deuren. Bewoner Dominique Desimpel is gefascineerd door oude huizen, kunstwerken, objecten en het licht dat hen tot leven wekt. In de San Marco werd hij verliefd op de antieke mozaïekvloeren. Uiteindelijk verhandelt hij oude en nieuwe vloeren, prachtige natuursteen en exquise materialen die mooi verouderen. De decoratie is natuurlijk van zijn hand. Als verzamelaar brengt hij mooie objecten bijeen. Voor de architectuur deed hij een beroep op bouwmeester Stéphane Boens. De patina's op de wanden zijn van Angèle Boddaert-Devletian en de decoratieve schildering naast de keuken van de Argentijn Pablo Piatti. Dominique hertekent regelmatig een stuk van zijn woning. Onlangs richtte hij de keuken opnieuw in en putte uit zijn collectie Napolitaanse vloertegels om het kookeiland te bekleden. De keuken van deze woning maakt trouwens deel uit van de ontvangst- en leefruimte. Daar hoort ook de blauwe bibliotheek bij.

INTIMITÉ

Musardant dans cet intérieur, on songe inévitablement aux tableaux de Pieter de Hooch, le maître hollandais du XVIIᵉ siècle avec ses merveilleux intérieurs à la lumière attendrissante. Cette même lumière s'instille dans cette maison avec des murs quasiment borgnes côté rue mais ouverte côté jardin. Encore que… Contrairement aux maisons contemporaines qui laissent simplement entrer l'extérieur par les grandes fenêtres, ici la frontière entre intérieur et extérieur est délicatement dosée par la disposition de hautes fenêtres et de petites portes. C'est que l'occupant, Dominique Desimpel, est fasciné par les maisons anciennes, les œuvres d'art, les objets et la lumière qui leur donne vie. À Saint-Marc, il est tombé amoureux des sols en mosaïque ancienne. Finalement, il s'est mis au commerce de sols anciens et modernes, de superbes pierres naturelles et des matériaux exquis qui vieillissent joliment. Collectionneur de beaux objets, il s'est évidemment occupé de la décoration. Mais il a fait appel à Stéphane Boens pour l'aspect architecture, à Angèle Boddaert-Devletian pour la patine sur les murs et à l'Argentin Pablo Piatti pour la peinture décorative à côté de la cuisine. Redessinant régulièrement une partie de la maison, Dominique vient de réaménager sa cuisine et se servant de sa collection de carreaux napolitains pour habiller le bloc cuisine. Cette cuisine fait d'ailleurs partie, tout comme la bibliothèque bleue, des espaces de réception et de la vie dans la maison.

INTIMATE

Walking through this interior inevitably brings to mind the superb interiors, with their soft and endearing light, painted by the seventeenth-century Dutch master Pieter de Hooch. The same light also finds its way into this house that is almost completely blind on the street side, but opens out on the garden side. But not like a contemporary home with large windows that let in the whole of the exterior. Here the boundary between inside and outside consists of studied and stylish combination of large windows and small doors. Its occupant Dominique Desimpel is fascinated by old houses, artworks, *objets* and the light that brings them to life. In San Marco he fell in love with antique mosaic floors. In fact he deals in old and new floors, beautiful natural stone and exquisite materials that age nicely. The decoration is of course by himself. As a collector he brings together beautiful objects. For the architecture he called in architect Stéphane Boens. The patinas on the walls are by Angèle Boddaert-Devletian and the decorative painting next to the kitchen by the Argentinian Pablo Piatti. Dominique regularly redesigns parts of his house. Recently he refurbished the kitchen, drawing from his collection of Neapolitan tiles to cover the cooking area. The kitchen here is an integral part of the reception and living area. This also includes the blue library.

De grote woonkamer is dus aan de straatzijde gesloten, waardoor de noordwand net een kamerscherm lijkt. Bovendien hangt er een antieke landkaart op, net zoals op de schilderijen van Vermeer. De kleuren, het licht en de verhoudingen verwijzen inderdaad naar de Hollandse interieurschilderingen van weleer. Hier en daar voeren hedendaagse accenten je terug naar onze tijd.

Le grand séjour est donc fermé côté rue de sorte que la paroi nord ressemble à un paravent. En plus, il s'y trouve une ancienne carte tout comme sur les tableaux de Vermeer. Et en effet, les couleurs, la lumière et les rapports sont absolument comme sur les tableaux d'intérieurs hollandais de jadis. Mais par-ci par-là, quelques éléments nous ramènent au présent.

With the big living room is closed to the street side, the north wall appears as a screen. On it hangs an antique map, as on Vermeer paintings. The colours, light and the proportions are indeed those of Dutch interior paintings of yesteryear. Here and there contemporary accents bring us back to the present day.

De keuken is een nieuwe creatie van Dominique Desimpel waarvoor hij antieke tegels in een hedendaagse context plaatste. Rechts zien we de ontvangstruimte met de bibliotheek, waarvan de muren in tintelend blauw zijn geborsteld: een hemelse tint. Dit is tevens het rariteitenkabinet van de woning. Uiteraard krijg je overal antieke tegels te bewonderen.

La cuisine est une nouvelle création de Dominique Desimpel qui a intégré des carreaux antiques dans un contexte contemporain. À droite, la pièce de réception avec la bibliothèque où les murs ont été peints dans un bleu étincelant : une teinte céleste. C'est en même temps le cabinet de curiosités de la demeure. Et il va de soi qu'on y admire un peu partout des carreaux antiques.

The kitchen is a new creation by Dominique Desimpel, setting antique tiles in a contemporary context. To the right we see the reception area with the bookcase, its walls painted a heavenly sparkling blue. This is also the curiosities cabinet of the house. Of course, everywhere are antique tiles to admire.

177

Een mysterieuze tussenruimte, tussen inkom en keuken, eventueel een kleine eetkamer, werd door de Argentijnse kunstenaar Pablo Piatti beschilderd met planten en vogels. Rechts vertoeven we in de gasten-kamer, waarvoor decoratieschilder Angèle Boddaert-Devletian een Gustaviaans decor actualiseerde. Voor de onderste plint werden antieke mangaankleurige tegels uit Neder-land gebruikt.

Un espace intermédiaire tant soit peu mystérieux entre le vestibule et la cuisine, à la rigueur une petite salle à manger, a été décoré de plantes et d'oiseaux par l'artiste argentin Pablo Piatti. À droite, on se retrouve dans la chambre d'amis avec un décor gustavien actualisé par la peintre-décoratrice Angèle Boddaert-Devletian. Pour la plinthe du bas, on est allé trouver des carreaux de couleur manganèse aux Pays-Bas.

A mysterious intermediate area, between the lobby and kitchen, maybe a small dining room, was painted with plants and birds by Argentine artist Pablo Piatti. To the right we are in the guest room for which decorator Angèle Boddaert-Devletian produced a Gustavian style décor. Antique manganese coloured tiles from the Netherlands have been used for the lower plinth.

Léonard de Vinci

POP ART

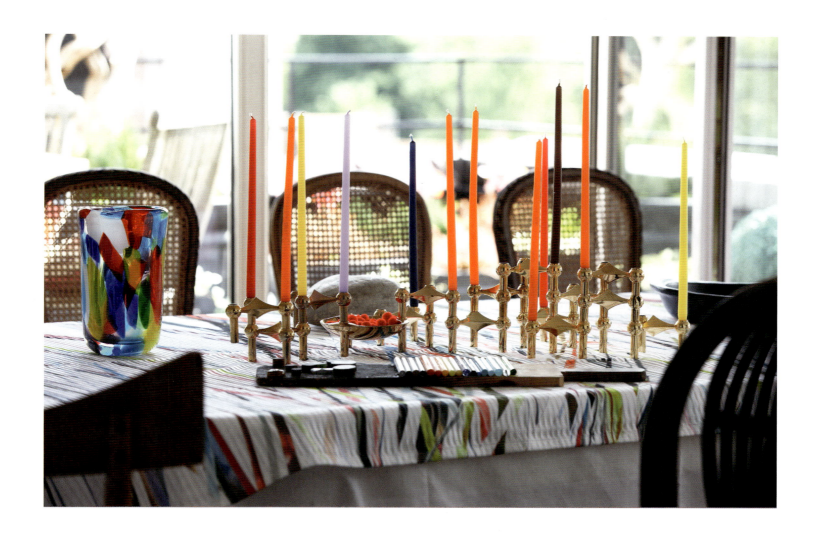

WONEN OP HET DAK

De Brusselse architect Caroline Notté heeft een tijdelijke pied-à-terre in Brussel, in de omgeving van het Georges Brugmannplein. Daar komt ze nu en dan wat werken en genieten van de gezellige buurt, die ze vanuit de flat vooral van bovenaf ziet. De woonruimte situeert zich op de bovenste verdieping van een art-decoflatgebouw. Het is een unieke belevenis om vanuit je woonkamer zowel de stad als de wolken te zien. Caroline Notté is als architect een buitenbeentje, onder meer omdat ze ook als artistiek fotograaf actief is. Ze maakt beelden van landschappen en gebouwen, die ze met licht als schilderijen aan de muur hangt. Maar ze verzamelt ook aardig wat kunst van andere beeldende kunstenaars. Ze vindt het boeiend om daartussen te werken. 'Ik koop van alles wat ik leuk vind en denk daar niet te veel over na', legt ze spontaan uit. Zoals ze zelf opmerkt, zijn veel moderne architecten tuk op strak uitgelijnde interieurs en verkiest ze zelf eerder toevallige 'kronkels'. Ze is weg van etnische kunst en ornamenten en vindt niet dat de omgeving waarin je leeft of werkt er zo serieus moet uitzien. 'Als architect ben je trouwens al de hele dag bezig met de controle van de perfectie', vertelt ze. Daarom is deze ruimte een beetje 'anticomputer' en humoristisch getint. Ze houdt van een surrealistische noot. In haar slaapkamer hangt trouwens een werk van Salvador Dalí en in de keuken een ingelijste jeansbroek van Andy Warhol.

HABITER SUR LE TOIT

L'architecte bruxelloise Caroline Notté possède un pied-à-terre temporaire à Bruxelles, dans les environs de la place Georges Brugmann. Elle vient y travailler de temps en temps tout en profitant de ce quartier convivial qu'elle aperçoit surtout du haut de son appartement. Cet espace de vie se situe en effet à l'étage supérieur d'un immeuble Art déco où elle profite pleinement de cette expérience unique d'apercevoir aussi bien la ville que les nuages à partir de son séjour. En tant qu'architecte, Caroline Notté est un personnage à part. Sans doute parce qu'elle s'adonne en même temps à la photographie artistique. Elle réalise des images de paysages et d'édifices qu'elle accroche avec un éclairage comme des tableaux au mur. Mais elle collectionne aussi pas mal d'œuvres d'art d'autres plasticiens, car elle trouve très passionnant de travailler dans leur proximité. « J'achète un peu de tout parmi ce qui me plaît sans trop y réfléchir », explique-t-elle spontanément. Comme elle l'observe aussi elle-même, beaucoup d'architectes modernes privilégient des intérieurs aux lignes austères alors qu'elle préfère plutôt des courbes fortuites. Elle adore l'art et les ornements ethniques et ne trouve pas que l'espace dans lequel on vit ou travaille doit avoir l'air si sérieux. « En tant qu'architecte, on s'occupe déjà toute la journée de contrôle de la perfection », dit-elle. C'est pourquoi cet espace a un petit air 'anti-ordinateur' et beaucoup d'humour. Elle n'est pas contre une touche de surréalisme non plus : elle a d'ailleurs une œuvre de Salvador Dalí dans sa chambre à coucher et un jean d'Andy Warhol encadré dans sa cuisine.

LIVING ON THE ROOF

Brussels architect Caroline Notté has a pied-à-terre in Brussels, near the Place Georges Brugmann. Here she comes now and then to work and to enjoy the cosy neighbourhood, seen in particular from above. The living room is on the top floor of an Art Deco apartment building. It is a unique experience to see both the city and the clouds from your living room. As an architect, Caroline Notté is something of an outsider, partly because she also works as an artist-photographer, creating images of landscapes and buildings which she hangs, lit like paintings, on the walls. But she also collects lots of art from other artists. She loves working surrounded by these pieces. "I buy everything I like and don't give too much thought to it", she says spontaneously. As she herself points out, many modern architects go for tightly aligned interiors, while she prefers a few accidental 'twists'. She is into ethnic art and ornaments and does not believe a living or working environment should look too serious. "As an architect you are busy all day controlling perfection", she says. For that reason this space is a bit 'anti-computer', with a streak of humour. She loves surrealist notes. Her bedroom contains a work by Salvador Dalí and her kitchen a framed pair of Andy Warhol's jeans.

Caroline Notté heeft bovenop een art-deco-gebouw in Brussel een tijdelijke pied-à-terre waar ze nu en dan logeert. Het decor is heel spontaan en speels. Ze ontwerpt als architect wel strakke gebouwen, maar houdt zelf van decors vol grappige en decoratieve accenten. Aan haar woning vol kunst en trouvailles voel je dat ze de wereld rondreist.

Caroline Notté dispose tout en haut d'un édifice Art déco à Bruxelles d'un pied-à-terre temporaire où elle loge de temps en temps. Le décor en est très spontané et enjoué. Si elle conçoit en tant qu'architecte des bâtiments aux lignes rigoureuses, elle adore les décors débordants d'accents comiques et décoratifs. Les objets d'art et les trouvailles dans sa maison révèlent bien qu'elle est une grande voyageuse.

Caroline Notté has a pied-à-terre at the top of an Art Deco building in Brussels where she occasionally stays. The décor is spontaneous and playful. As an architect she designs more clean-lined buildings, but is herself fond of décors with lots of amusing and decorative accents. From her home full of art and *trouvailles* you sense that this is a woman who travels the world.

Deze plek is een persoonlijke reactie tegen de al te afgemeten wereld waarin we leven. Het lijkt een allegaartje, maar wie aandachtig rondkijkt, merkt al gauw dat al deze objecten en meubels hier niet per toeval zijn beland. Er zitten ook onverwachte souvenirs bij, zoals de driehoek, een fragment van de originele buitenwand van het Atomium in Brussel.

Cet endroit constitue une réaction personnelle à l'univers bien trop encadré dans lequel nous vivons. S'il a un peu l'air d'un bric-à-brac, un regard plus attentif révèle que tous ces objets et ces meubles ne se retrouvent pas là par hasard. On y tombe aussi sur des souvenirs inattendus comme ce grand triangle, un morceau du mur extérieur d'origine de l'Atomium à Bruxelles.

This place is a personal reaction against the overly measured world in which we live. At first sight it's a jumble, but look around carefully and you find that none of these objects and furniture ended up here by chance. There are also unexpected souvenirs, such as the triangular fragment of the original outer skin of the Brussels Atomium.

De zetel opgebouwd uit geweien bezorgt dit interieur een dosis antidesign, net zoals de kleurrijke kussens die overal rondslingeren. Caroline Notté houdt immers van een bont palet en vindt dat de plekken waar ze vertoeft het best de sfeer van een vakantiewoning uitstralen.

Le siège composé de bois de cerf donne à cet intérieur une bonne dose d'anti-design. Tout comme les coussins multicolores disséminés un peu partout. Affectionnant en effet une palette bariolée, Caroline Notté estime que les endroits où elle demeure peuvent bien baigner dans une ambiance de maison de vacances.

The chair made of antlers gives this home a dose of anti-design. As do the brightly coloured cushions lying around everywhere. Caroline Notté loves a bright palette and likes the places where she lives to have the feeling of a holiday home about them.

AMSTER-DAM

TUSSEN OOST, ZUID EN WEST

De ontwerper San Ming betrekt al jaren een flat in Amsterdam-Zuid. Hij bewoont hetzelfde appartement, maar gooit tweemaal per jaar alles buiten voor een volledig nieuwe aankleding. Dan wordt alles aan vrienden en kennissen verkocht. Daar oogst hij tot ver over de grenzen succes mee. Ming kreeg ooit een mode-opleiding, maar gooide zich snel op het interieur. Hij richt van alles in, tot en met boten. Na de verkoop begint hij opnieuw met stofferen. Hij zoekt meubels, objecten en kunstwerken. Maar hij doet veel zelf, ook kunstwerken maken. Zijn woning is tevens zijn atelier. De stijl van San Ming evolueert, maar er schuilt wel een constante lijn in. Hij houdt van constructivistische architectuur en kunst, een beetje à la De Stijl. Hij is ook tuk op klassieke moderne kunstenaars en designers als Robert Motherwell, George Nakashima en Isamu Noguchi. Voor zijn inspiratie grabbelt hij zowel in de ton van de Japanse cultuur als in die van de Chinese en Afrikaanse. Dit combineert hij met Westerse vormgeving. Hij begrijpt niet waarom mensen hun interieur niet snel grondig veranderen. Volgens hem doet een nieuw interieur je herleven. 'Wat ik doe, is waar veel mensen over dromen, maar niet durven', zegt San Ming. Hij vindt woonkeukens totaal onaantrekkelijk en vindt ook de overdreven aandacht voor badkamers overbodig. Voor hem is de living room de centrale plek waar alles gebeurt.

ENTRE ORIENT, SUD ET OCCIDENT

Le créateur San Ming habite depuis de nombreuses années un appartement à Amsterdam-Zuid. Deux fois par an, il flanque tout à la porte et entame une décoration entièrement renouvelée. Il vend tout à des amis ou des relations, ce qui lui assure du coup un succès considérable jusque loin au-delà des frontières. Ayant suivi une formation de mode, Ming s'est très vite tourné vers la décoration. Il aménage plein de choses, y compris des bateaux. Une fois qu'il a tout vendu, il recommence l'habillage de son appartement et cherche pour cela des meubles, des objets et des œuvres d'art. Mais il réalise aussi beaucoup lui-même, y compris des œuvres d'art. Sa maison est donc aussi son atelier. Si le style de Ming évolue, on y reconnaît quand même une constante : il aime l'architecture et l'art constructivistes, un peu dans le genre De Stijl. Il affectionne aussi les artistes et créateurs modernes classiques tels que Robert Motherwell, Georges Nakashima et Isamu Noguchi. Pour son inspiration, il fouille aussi bien dans la culture japonaise que dans celle d'Afrique et de Chine et combine ces éléments avec le stylisme occidental. Il ne comprend en fait pas pourquoi les gens ne changent pas rapidement leur intérieur. À ses yeux, un nouvel intérieur fait aussi revivre. Ce que je fais, dit San Ming, c'est ce dont beaucoup de gens rêvent sans oser s'y risquer. Les cuisines américaines ne sont pas du tout son truc et il trouve superflue l'attention exagérée accordée à la salle d'eau. Pour lui, le séjour est l'endroit central où se déroule l'essentiel.

BETWEEN EAST, SOUTH AND WEST

Designer San Ming has for many years occupied in a flat in Amsterdam-South. He lives in the same apartment, but twice a year throws everything out, selling it to friends and acquaintances and starting again from scratch. This has made him successful well beyond the Netherlands. Ming once trained in fashion, but rapidly threw himself into interior design. He decorates everything, including boats. After the sale he starts furnishing all over again, looking for furniture, objects and artworks. But a lot he does himself, including artworks. His home is also his studio. San Ming's style is an evolving one, but there is a constant line in it. He loves constructivist architecture and art, a bit *à la* De Stijl. He is also keen on classic modern artists and designers like Robert Motherwell, George Nakashima and Isamu Noguchi. For inspiration, he draws from Japanese, as well as Chinese and African culture. This he combines with Western design. He does not understand why people do not change their interiors regularly and radically. For San Ming, a new interior revives you. "I do what many people dream about but lack the courage to do", he says. He finds kitchen-living rooms totally unattractive and the exaggerated attention paid to bathrooms superfluous. For him, the living room is the central location where everything happens.

Ooit was dit zijn zitkamer, nu heeft San Ming er een werkruimte van gemaakt. Eigenlijk is dit zijn leefruimte, waar hij de meeste tijd doorbrengt. Ditmaal lijkt de ruimte op een kunstgalerie. Door de luiken voor de ramen waan je je in een hedendaags gebouw, maar dat is niet zo.

Ce qui fut un jour son salon, San Ming l'a transformé actuellement en espace de travail. Mais c'est en fait son espace de vie car il y passe la plupart de son temps. Cette fois, l'espace a l'air d'une galerie d'art. Grâce aux volets devant les fenêtres, on a l'impression de se trouver dans un immeuble contemporain, ce qui n'est pas du tout le cas.

This was once his living room, now San Ming has turned it into a workspace. Actually, this is his living space where he spends the majority of his time. This time the space resembles an art gallery. The slats in front of this window suggest this is a modern building, but that's not so.

De flat van San Ming huist in een vooroorlogs flatgebouw in Amsterdam. Maar binnen denk je in een Parijse art gallery uit de jaren zestig te vertoeven. Hij heeft een zwak voor constructivistische structuren en houdt van abstracte kunst die knipoogt naar De Stijl.

L'appartement de San Ming se trouve dans un immeuble d'avant-guerre à Amsterdam. Mais à l'intérieur, on se croirait dans une galerie d'art parisienne des années soixante. San a un faible pour des structures constructivistes et adore l'art abstrait qui adresse un clin d'œil au courant artistique De Stijl.

San Ming's apartment is in a pre-war building in Amsterdam. But inside you'd think you were in a 1960s Paris art gallery. Ming has a weakness for constructivist structures and loves abstract art that tips a wink at De Stijl.

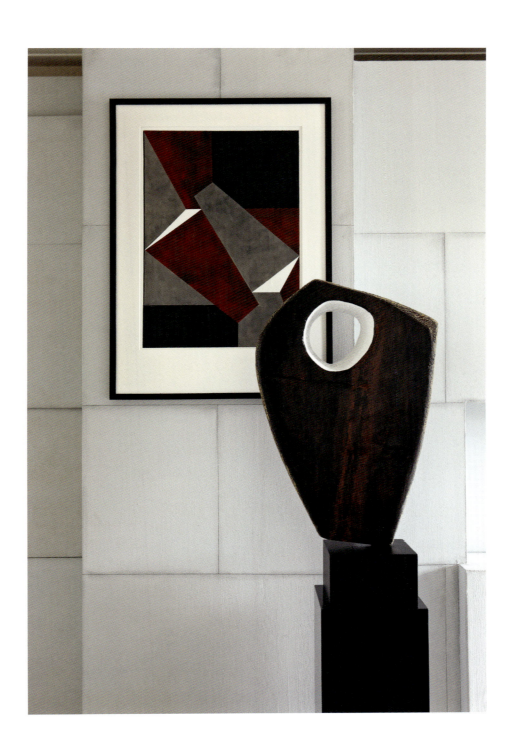

Zelfs de slaapkamer zit vol zwart-witcontrasten, zoals je die in Amsterdam wel veel ziet. Dit zorgt voor een uitgesproken grafische stijl. Ming richt zijn flat dus ongeveer tweemaal per jaar opnieuw in en vervaardigt speciaal daarvoor telkens een reeks kunstwerken. Alles wordt nadien verkocht aan verzamelaars van zijn stijl.

Même la chambre à coucher est dominée par les contrastes noir et blanc qu'on retrouve assez fréquemment à Amsterdam et qui donnent aux pièces un style explicitement graphique. Ming réaménage donc son appartement deux fois par an et réalise à chaque fois une série d'œuvres d'art à cet effet. Il les vend ensuite à des collectionneurs de son style.

Even the bedroom is full of the black and white contrasts you see a lot of in Amsterdam. This creates a distinctly graphic style. Ming redesigns his apartment about twice a year, creating each time a special sequence of artworks for it. Almost everything is then sold to collectors of his style.

ROCK & ROLL

ROCK & ROLL

Meestal wordt voor de inrichting van een woonruimte vooral rekening gehouden met de lichtinval en de ruimte zelf. Zelden wordt de stijl bepaald door een indirect element. Toch is dat hier wel het geval. De bewoners, die altijd al tuk waren op stijlvolle vintage, konden hun interieur best zelf inrichten, maar voor de oplossing van een aantal praktische problemen kwamen ze terecht bij meubelontwerper Filip Janssens. In deze open woonruimte moest niet alleen de televisie, maar ook de muziekinstallatie met een oude platenspeler worden verstopt. Filip Janssens bedacht daarvoor een vrij unieke wandkast, opgebouwd uit op elkaar gestapelde houten dozen, meestal voorzien van deurtjes. Ze werden als een puzzel ineengevlochten tot een prachtige constructivistische wand die visueel veel aandacht trekt en de flat meteen een identiteit schenkt. Voorts is de aankleding van deze handig geconcipieerde flat verfrissend, met een combinatie van oude en nieuwe spullen. De bewoners houden van originele lampen, zoals de bloemvormige Pistillo aan de wand en de Pipistrello van Gae Aulenti, stuk voor stuk iconen uit de sixties. In de door Janssens ontworpen platenkast zitten trouwens de bijpassende platen uit die tijd. Ook de grote witte zit, net een Amerikaanse slee, heeft iets rock & roll.

ROCK & ROLL

La plupart du temps, on tient surtout compte de la lumière et de l'espace même pour l'aménagement d'un séjour et beaucoup plus rarement d'un élément indirect qui viendrait en définir le style. C'est pourtant ce qui s'est passé ici. Amoureux de vintage de qualité, les habitants étaient parfaitement capables de décorer eux-mêmes leur intérieur, mais pour résoudre une série de questions pratiques, ils se sont adressés au styliste de meubles Filip Janssens. Il était notamment question de cacher dans ce séjour ouvert non seulement une télé mais aussi une sono avec un vieux tourne-disque. Filip Janssens a imaginé pour cela un placard fort original composé d'un empilement de boîtes en bois, la plupart du temps munies de portes. Encastrées à la manière d'un puzzle, elles constituent une superbe paroi constructiviste qui attire fortement l'attention visuelle et procure une identité à cet appartement. Avec sa combinaison d'objets anciens et nouveaux, le reste de la décoration donne à cet appartement bien pratique un air de fraîcheur. Les habitants aiment par exemple les lampes originales, comme la Pistillo en forme de fleur au mur et la Pipistrello de Gae Aulenti, de véritables icônes des années soixante. Précisons encore que le placard conçu par Janssens prévoit également le rangement des disques de cette époque. Il y a aussi le grand siège blanc avec son air de belle américaine qui dégage une ambiance de rock & roll.

ROCK & ROLL

In most cases the primary elements in designing a living area are the incident light and the space itself. Only rarely is the style determined by an indirect element. This is one of these rare cases. The residents who had always been keen on stylish vintage interior were perfectly capable of organizing their interior themselves, but turned to furniture designer Filip Janssens for solutions to a number of practical problems. This open living area needed to contain not just a television, but also a sound system including an old gramophone turntable. For this Filip Janssens came up with a rather unique cabinet consisting of stacked wooden boxes, most of them fitted with doors. These were then interwoven like a jigsaw puzzle to form a superb and attention-grabbing constructivist wall that immediately bestows an identity on the apartment. The decoration of this neatly conceived apartment is a refreshing combination of old and new. Its occupants love original lamps, like the flower-shaped Pistillo on the wall and the Pipistrello by Gae Aulenti, all icons from the sixties. In the record cabinet designed by Janssens are the matching records from that time. The big white limo-like chair has something rock & roll about it.

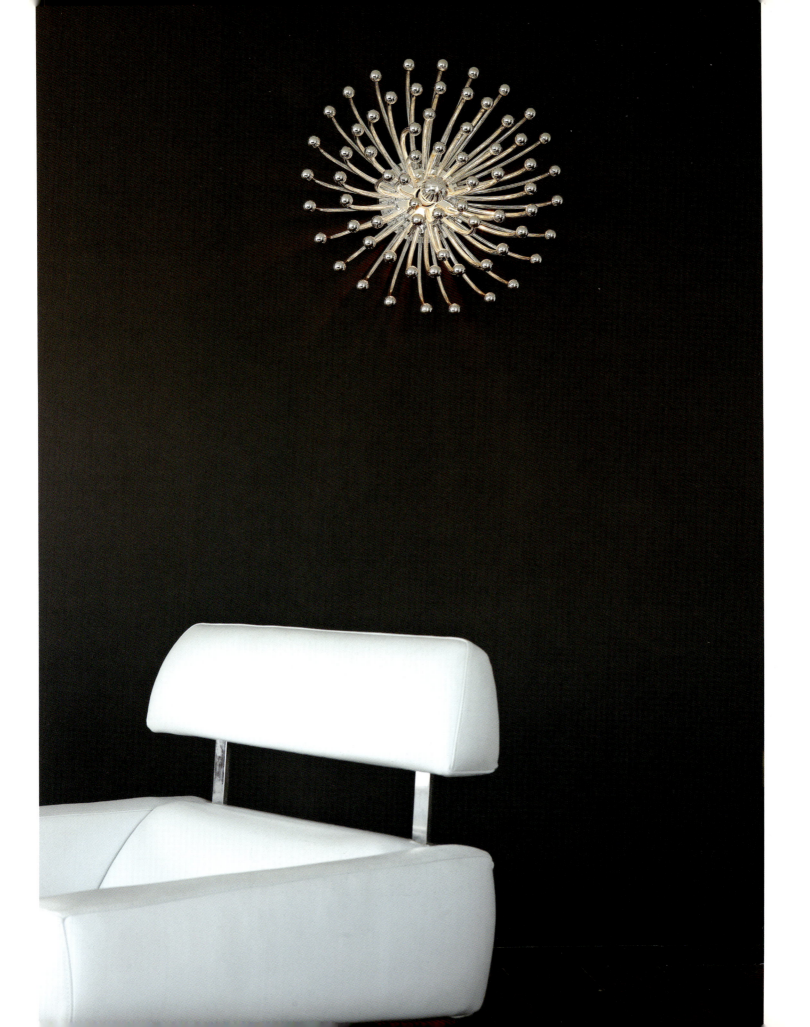

Deze flat is trendy en toch ietwat klassiek door de rustige en evenwichtige aankleding. Er staat ook heel wat authentiek vintage, zoals de eettafel en stoelen van Eero Saarinen. De bewoners houden van design met een organische vorm. Zo lijkt de Pistello-lamp aan de muur op een zeeanemoon.

Cet appartement très à la mode a en même temps une touche classique par sa décoration calme et équilibrée. On y trouve aussi beaucoup de vintage authentique comme la table à manger et les chaises d'Eero Saarinen. Les habitants adorent le design aux formes organiques. L'applique de Pistello, par exemple, ressemble à une anémone de mer.

This apartment is trendy and yet somewhat classical with its calm and balanced decoration. There are also lots of authentic vintage pieces, like the Eero Saarinen dining table and chairs. The inhabitants love organically-shaped design. The Pistello lamp on the wall looks like a sea anemone.

Meubelontwerper Filip Janssens ontwierp de wandkast, opgebouwd uit een puzzel van dozen. Daarin zitten onder meer het televisietoestel, een oude platenspeler en een collectie platen verstopt. Deze flat huist in een mooi gebouw, ontworpen door architectenbureau a154, met een eenvoudige structuur en verschuifbare houten schermen die het licht doseren.

Ce placard composé d'un puzzle de boîtes est une création du créateur de mobilier Filip Janssens. Il abrite entre autres le téléviseur, un vieux tourne-disque et une collection de disques. L'appartement fait partie d'un bel édifice dessiné par le bureau d'architects a154, avec une structure toute simple et des parois en bois coulissantes qui permettent de doser la lumière.

Furniture designer Filip Janssens designed the cupboard, consisting of of jigsaw of boxes. Hidden in it are, among others, the television, an old record player and a collection of gramophone records. This apartment is housed in an attractive building, designed by architect's firm a154, with a simple structure and sliding wooden screens that serve to dose the light.

ATTIC

LOFT OP ZOLDER

Oude zolders mogen dan nog zo mooi zijn, wat je ermee kunt aanvangen ligt niet altijd voor de hand. 'Het is niet evident om er een woonruimte van te maken', weet architect Pieter Vandenhout, die deze zolderloft in Diest onlangs vormgaf. Het is een zolder van 185 m² oppervlakte boven het voormalige abdiskwartier van een oud klooster. Het gebouw verkeerde in slechte staat, maar het zeventiende-eeuwse eiken gebinte, net een omgekeerd schip, was nog goed en het herstellen meer dan waard. Zolders zijn mooi, maar donker, wat een nadeel is voor een woonruimte. Om het licht op een elegante manier naar binnen te brengen, werden glasvlakken tussen de balken aangebracht, waardoor er een soort ateliersfeer werd gecreëerd. Deze vlakken zorgen voor indirect licht. Er kwamen dus geen dakvensters of klapramen. De flat heeft een open leefruimte die doorloopt tot de slaaphoek. Deze zit evenwel verstopt achter de natte cel, die als een geïsoleerde doos in de ruimte staat en het gebinte niet aanraakt. Naast de zithoek bracht Pieter Vandenhout een hedendaags terras aan, dat eigenlijk het hart van de woning is. Het is de plek waar iedereen overdag het liefst vertoeft. Om de donkerheid van het gebinte te verlichten, koos de ontwerper voor veel wit. De vloeren zijn van bijna witte kalkmortel en ook veel meubels zijn wit. Dit resulteert in een subtiele weerkaatsing van het licht.

LOFT AU GRENIER

S'il existe de superbes vieux greniers, il n'est pas toujours évident d'en faire quelque chose de valeur. Surtout pas de le transformer en espace de vie, comme le sait bien l'architecte Pieter Vandenhout qui vient de réaliser ce grenier-loft à Diest. Il s'agit d'un grenier avec une surface de 185 m² au sol au-dessus des quartiers de l'abbesse dans un ancien couvent. L'édifice même était en mauvais état, mais la charpente du XVIIᵉ siècle en chêne, pareille à un vaisseau inversé, était encore bonne et valait amplement une réhabilitation. Les greniers peuvent être très beaux, mais ils sont en général sombres et cela ne constitue pas un atout pour des espaces de vie. Afin de faire entrer la lumière avec élégance, des panneaux de verre ont été posés entre les poutres, créant ainsi une sorte d'ambiance d'atelier. Produisant un éclairage indirect, ils rendaient superflus lucarnes, fenêtres à tabatière ou autres œils-de-bœuf. L'habitation présente un séjour ouvert qui se prolonge jusqu'à l'espace à coucher, caché derrière une salle d'eau placée comme une boîte isolée dans l'espace, ne touchant même pas la charpente. À côté du coin salon, Pieter Vandenhout a aménagé une terrasse contemporaine, en fait le cœur de l'habitation. Car c'est l'endroit où tout un chacun préfère se tenir pendant la journée. Afin d'alléger les teintes sombres de la charpente, le créateur a introduit beaucoup de blanc. Les sols ont un revêtement de gâchis quasiment blanc et une bonne partie des meubles sont également blancs. Il en résulte une réverbération subtile de la lumière.

LOFT IN THE ATTIC

Old attics may be beautiful, but are not always easy to convert. The difficulty of making living space out of them is all too familiar to architect Pieter Vandenhout, who recently designed this attic apartment in Diest. It is a 185 square metre loft area above the abbess's quarters of a former convent. The building was in poor condition, but the seventeenth-century oak truss roof, like an inverted ship, was still solid and more than worth restoring. Attics are beautiful, but dark, which is a disadvantage for a living area. To bring light into the loft in an elegant way, panes of glass were placed between the beams, creating a kind of studio atmosphere. These panes provide indirect light, without dormer windows or skylights. The flat has an open living room that extends through to the sleeping area. This is secluded behind the kitchen and bathroom that sit together like an insulated box without touching the roof supports. Next to the sitting area, Pieter Vandenhout has added a contemporary terrace, which is really the heart of the house, and where everyone likes to hang out during the day. To lighten the darkness of the rafters, he has opted for lots of white. The floors are in almost white lime mortar and many pieces of furniture are white too, resulting in a subtle reflection of light.

Het zestiende-eeuwse gebinte bleef intact, en werd slechts aan de tuinzijde doorbroken met een witte doos die toegang verschaft tot een terras. Aan de andere zijde werd een rij pannen vervangen door glasplaten die prachtig licht doorlaten. De flat is één open ruimte waarin enkele losse witte wanden staan. De witte vloer zorgt voor extra licht. De slaapruimte zit achter de natte cel, die in een witte doos zit vervat.

La charpente du XVIᵉ siècle est demeurée intacte et n'a été interrompue que du côté jardin par une boîte blanche donnant accès à la terrasse. De l'autre côté, une série de tuiles ont été remplacées par des plaques de verre qui laissent entrer une superbe lumière. Le sol blanc augmente d'ailleurs aussi la luminosité. L'espace chambre à coucher se cache derrière la salle d'eau aménagée dans une boîte blanche.

The sixteenth-century truss roof remained intact, broken through only on the garden side with a white box that provides access to a terrace. On part of the other side, the tiling has been replaced by glass panes that let in a superb light. The apartment is a single open space broken up by free-standing white walls. The white floor provides additional light. The sleeping area is behind the white box containing the shower cabinet.

LONDON

215

EEN LONDENS KLEURENPALET

Joa Studholme, de kleurenconsulent van de beroemde Britse verffabrikant Farrow & Ball, betrekt een ruim pand in de buurt van Portobello Road in Londen. Het is uiteraard een kleurrijke woning. Hier kan ze naar hartenlust experimenteren met kleuren. Joa is voor de fabrikant wat de neus is voor een parfumhuis. Ze ontwikkelt kleurcollecties en zet ook nieuwe trends uit. Haar palet is typisch Brits, met veel verschillende tonen van wit, blauw en groen. Grijze of witte interieurs vindt ze minder spannend. Haar stijlvolle Victoriaanse woning is van net voor de Eerste Wereldoorlog. Het pand zit vol paneeldeuren, lambriseringen, mooie schouwen en rijke stucplafonds. De stijl is klassiek, maar de aankleding modern. De inkom schilderde ze donker, als contrast met de rest van de woning. Het is leuk om van een duistere gang een kleurrijke kamer binnen te stappen. Volgens haar versterken donkere tinten de intimiteit en werken ze relaxerend. Lichtblauw en groen vindt ze beter passen voor een slaapruimte. Voor een woonkamer stelt ze donkerrood voor, een kleur die vooral 's avonds schittert. Ze combineert deze tinten altijd met wit voor vloeren, deuren en lambriseringen. Ze haalt ook inspiratie uit de kunst. In haar woonkamer hangen zeefdrukken van de Schots-Ierse kunstschilder William Scott, die subtiele kleurcombinaties borstelde. Je voelt meteen dat dit een huis is waar veel vrienden over de vloer komen. De kleuren en vele objecten zorgen voor een gastvrije sfeer.

A LONDON COLOUR PALETTE

Joa Studholme, colour consultant to famous British paint manufacturer Farrow & Ball, lives in a large property near London's Portobello Road. It is, needless to say, a colourful home. Here she can experiment with colours to her heart's content. Joa is for the paint manufacturer what a nose is for a perfume house. She develops colour collections and sets new trends. Her palette is typically British, with multiple shades of white, blue and green. Grey or white interiors she finds less exciting. Her elegant Victorian house, built just before the First World War, is full of panel doors, wainscoting, attractive fireplaces, and rich stucco ceilings. The style is classical, but the decoration modern. The entrance she has painted dark to contrast with the rest of the house: it's pleasant to step from a dark hallway into a colourful room. For her, darker tones strengthen intimacy and have a relaxing effect, while light blue and green are better in a bedroom. For a living room she proposes dark red, a colour that gleams especially at night. These colours she combines always with white for floors, doors and panelling. She also draws inspiration from art. Her living room contains screenprints by Scottish-Irish painter William Scott who produced subtle colour combinations with his brush. You immediately feel this is a house that lots of friends pass through. The colours and many objects provide a welcoming atmosphere.

UNE PALETTE LONDONIENNE

Conseillère en couleurs pour le célèbre fabricant de couleurs britannique Farrow & Ball, Joa Studholme habite une grande maison dans les environs de Portobello Road à Londres. On ne s'étonne pas qu'il s'agisse d'une demeure haute en couleurs qui lui permet d'ailleurs d'expérimenter à volonté. Joa joue pour le fabricant de couleurs un rôle comparable à celui du 'nez' pour un parfumeur. Elle développe des collections de couleurs et lance de nouvelles tendances. Avec sa palette typiquement britannique qui propose une grande variété de blancs, verts et bleus, elle trouve les intérieurs blancs ou gris moins passionnants. Sa maison d'un beau style victorien datant de juste avant la Première Guerre mondiale, regorge de portes à panneaux, de lambris, de belles cheminées et de riches plafonds en stuc. Si le style est classique, l'habillement est résolument moderne. Ainsi a-t-elle peint l'entrée en couleurs sombres en contraste avec le reste de la maison. Pour elles, les teintes sombres renforcent l'intimité tout en ayant un effet relaxant. Pour les chambres à coucher, elle suggère plutôt le bleu clair et le vert, tandis qu'un rouge sombre dans le séjour donne surtout beaucoup de brillance en soirée. Elle associe toujours ces couleurs avec du blanc pour les sols, les portes et les lambris. S'inspirant également de l'art, elle a accroché dans son séjour des sérigraphies de l'artiste peintre écossais-irlandais William Scott qui a peint de subtiles combinaisons de couleurs. Bref, on sent tout de suite qu'on est dans une maison où passent de nombreux amis. Les couleurs et les nombreux objets créent une ambiance très accueillante.

In dit Victoriaans huis ligt de keuken, met laag plafond, onder de grote woonkamer met bibliotheek. Hoewel Joa Studholme tuk is op een rijk palet, schilderde ze de bibliotheek effen, precies om extra aandacht te geven aan de boeken en objecten. De aankleding is klassiek, maar de kleuren zijn van deze tijd.

Dans cette maison victorienne, la cuisine au plafond relativement bas, est située sous le grand séjour avec la bibliothèque. Bien qu'elle raffole d'une palette haute en couleurs, Joa Studholme a donné à cette bibliothèque une teinte unie pour mieux faire ressortir les livres et les objets. Si l'habillage est classique, les couleurs sont très contemporaines.

The low-ceilinged kitchen in this Victorian house lies underneath the large living room with its built-in bookcase. Although Joa Studholme loves a rich palette, she painted the bookcase in a single colour, precisely in order to set off the books and *objets d'art*. The décor is classical, but the colours contemporary.

In de woonkamer verwijzen de kleuren ontegensprekelijk naar het werk van de Britse kunstschilder William Scott, van wie er prints aan de muur hangen. Joa vindt veel inspiratie voor haar kleurenpalet in de moderne kunst.

Dans le séjour, les couleurs évoquent indéniablement l'œuvre de l'artiste peintre britannique William Scott dont quelques œuvres sont accrochées au mur. Pour sa palette de couleurs, Joa se laisse volontiers inspirer par l'art moderne.

In the living room the colours refer unambiguously to the work of British artist William Scott, prints of whose hang on the wall. Joa finds lots of inspiration for her colour palette in modern art.

ART
NOUVEAU

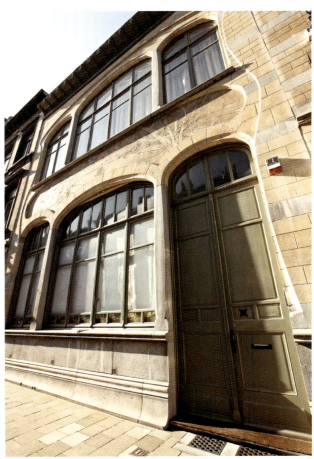

MET EEN ITALIAANSE TOETS

Dit ruime huis in Brussel werd in 1904 opgetrokken voor kunstenares Louise De Hem, die grote portretten schilderde. Het is een atelierwoning met metershoge plafonds en een subtiele lichtinval. Louise studeerde in Parijs en pendelde lang tussen de Franse hoofdstad en Brussel, waar ze zich uiteindelijk vestigde. Brussel was begin twintigste eeuw echt de hoofdstad van de art nouveau in West-Europa. Ze liet het huis ontwerpen door Ernest Blérot, naast Victor Horta een van dé vertegenwoordigers van de zweepslagstijl. Nu woont Elena Barenghi hier. Ze groeide op in Zwitserland, studeerde literatuur in Rome en New York en belandde uiteindelijk in de Europese hoofdstad. Ondertussen ging ze schilderen, fotograferen en woningen inrichten. Haar eigen woning telt verschillende spectaculaire leefruimten. Beneden heb je de ruime zitkamer, vroeger de expositieruimte van Louise De Hem. Het meer dan zes meter hoge plafond liet de bouw van een mezzanine toe voor een werkhoek. De Brusselse architect Pierre Lhoas tekende de metalen haard en de balustrade. Hij koos voor een moderne, industriële stijl, verwant aan de vormgeving van de Luikse art-nouveau-ontwerper Gustave Serrurier-Bovy. Deze stijl past perfect bij de woning. Het interieur oogt fris, met witte wanden en wat vintage. Het is clean noch kil van stijl. Elena houdt van strak Scandinavisch design en de industriële ontwerpen van Jean Prouvé.

UNE TOUCHE ITALIENNE

Cette maison spacieuse a été construite en 1904 à Bruxelles p[...] tiste Louise De Hem, peintre de grands portraits. C'est une [...] atelier avec de très hauts plafonds et une lumière subtile. Fai[...] études à Paris, Louise a longtemps fait la navette entre la ca[...] çaise et Bruxelles où elle s'est finalement installée. Au débu[...] siècle, Bruxelles était vraiment la capitale de l'Art nouveau [...] occidentale. Pour le concept de sa maison, elle a fait appel [...] rot, tout comme Victor Horta un des tout grands représent[...] ligne en 'coup de fouet'. Actuellement, la maison est occup[...] Barenghi qui, ayant grandi en Suisse, a étudié la littérature [...] New York avant de se fixer dans la capitale européenne. E[...] elle s'était mise à peindre, à faire de la photo et de la déco[...] rieur. Sa propre maison compte plusieurs espaces de vie [...] notamment le très spacieux séjour qui fut jadis l'espace [...] Louise De Hem. Avec un plafond de plus de 6 m de ha[...] indiqué d'aménager un coin de travail en mezzanine[...] le balcon sont de la main de l'architecte bruxellois [...] choisi un style industriel moderne, proche du sty[...] veau liégeois Gustave Serrurier-Bovy. Un style qui [...] ment à cette maison. L'intérieur dégage beaucoup [...] murs blancs et un peu de vintage, mais le style n'es[...] froid. Elena affectionne la rigueur du design scand[...] industrielles de Jean Prouvé.

WITH AN ITALIAN TOUCH

This spacious Brussels house was built in 1904 fo[...] Hem who painted large portraits. It is a studio ho[...]gs and subtle lighting. Louise studied in Paris and fo[...]ed between there and Brussels, where she finally setti[...]n the early 20th century the real capital of Art Nouv[...]u-rope. De Hem had the house designed by Ernest B[...] Victor Horta was one of the leading representatives o[...]yle. Elena Barenghi now lives here. She grew up in Swi[...]d literature in Rome and New York and ended up in th[...]ital. Meanwhile, she took up painting, photography and [...]ration. Her own home contains several spectacular living[...]tairs is the spacious living room, formerly Louise De He[...] area. The more than six metres high ceiling allowed for t[...]on of a mezzanine work area. Belgian architect Pierre Lhoa[...] the metal fireplace and the balustrade, opting for a modern, in[...]yle related to the work of Liège Art Nouveau designer Gustave S[...]Bovy. This style is perfect for the home. The interior looks fresh, [...]hite walls and a little vintage, clean without being cold. Elena loves [...]ek Scandinavian design and the industrial designs of Jean Prouvé.

Van het vroegere art-nouveau-interieur bleef er niet veel bewaard. Voor de voormalige expo-ruimte, thans living room van Elena Barenghi, ontwierp architect Pierre Lhoas een mezzanine met een industrieel ogende trap en haard, een beetje geïnspireerd op de stijl van Gustave Serrurier-Bovy. In deze ruimte verdeelt een doorzichtige bibliotheek (De Padova) de ruimte tussen zithoek en eethoek.

Il ne reste pas grand-chose de l'ancien intérieur Art nouveau. Pour le séjour d'Elena Barenghi qui fut jadis un espace d'exposition, l'architecte Pierre Lhoas a imaginé une mezzanine avec un escalier d'allure industrielle et une cheminée où on pourrait reconnaître une influence du style de Gustave Serrurier-Bovy. Dans cet espace, une bibliothèque transparente (De Padova) divise l'espace en coin salon et coin salle à manger.

Not much remained of the former Art Nouveau interior. For the former exhibition area, now Elena Barenghi's living room, architect Pierre Lhoas designed a mezzanine with an industrial-looking staircase and fireplace, a little inspired by the style of Gustave Serrurier-Bovy. Here a see-through bookcase (De Padova) divides the the space between sitting and dining areas.

Dit is het spannende zicht dat
je van bovenaf krijgt vanop
de mezzanine op de zithoek.
Zoiets kan natuurlijk alleen als
het plafond voldoende hoog is.
Hier is de hoogte ruim zes meter.
In dit huis geniet je niet alleen
van de dwarse, de diagonale,
maar ook van enkele verticale
perspectieven, en dat is hoogst
uitzonderlijk.

Telle est la vue plongeante
passionnante à partir de la
mezzanine sur le coin salon.
Évidemment, il faut pour cela
une hauteur sous plafond
suffisante et avec une hauteur
de plus de six mètres, cette
maison offre non seulement des
perspectives transversales ou
diagonales, mais des perspectives verticales extrêmement
rares dans les habitations privées.

This is the exciting view you
get from the mezzanine over
the sitting area. This is possible
of course only if the ceiling is
sufficiently high; here it is over six
metres. This provides the highly
unusual feature of a number of
vertical perspectives, in addition
to the transverse, diagonal ones.

ECLECTIC

ECLECTIC

Deze woonruimtes vinden we in een laatmiddeleeuws landhuis nabij Brugge. Het pand ligt naast het achttiende-eeuwse kasteel Rooigem, maar is veel ouder dan het kasteel zelf. Het is een typisch Vlaams bakstenen bouwwerk met een vrij robuuste architectuur zonder veel of grote vensters. Het oogt dus wat gesloten, zeker aan de buitenkant. Het werd helemaal opgeknapt door de antiquairs Jean-Philippe Demeyer, Frank Ver Elst en Jean-Paul Dewever, die niet alleen originele oudheden en moderniteiten zoeken, maar ook woningen inrichten in een eclectische stijl. Hun stijl evolueerde in de loop van de jaren tot een bonte leefwereld vol excentrieke objecten en veel kleur. Ze zijn ook niet bang voor rijke of hier en daar zelfs wat kitscherige accenten, waardoor hun interieur toch iets heeft van een theaterdecor. Rond het binnenplein van het landhuis hebben ze verschillende zit- en leefruimtes gecreëerd. De oranjerie is heel landelijk en ontspannend en in de tuinkamer waan je je eerder in de grootstad. De combinatie van wat eclectische vintage met oude muren werkt verfrissend. Ze hebben, een beetje op hun manier, de receptuur van David Nightingale Hicks, de beroemde Engelse decorateur, geactualiseerd met speelse noten. Hun stijl is helemaal van deze tijd en toch niet zo opdringerig als vele zogenaamd hedendaagse creaties. In tegenstelling tot veel moderne designers en architecten die vasthouden aan hun stijl en bang zijn voor veel stoffering, gaan deze antiquairs hier voluit met de decoratie.

ÉCLECTIQUE

On trouve ces pièces d'habitation dans un manoir datant du bas Moyen Âge près de Bruges. Jouxtant le château de Rooigem du xviiie siècle, il est donc nettement plus ancien que ce dernier. Il s'agit d'une construction en briques typiquement flamande avec une solide architecture et de rares fenêtres de surcroît pas très grandes. Il a donc l'air plutôt fermé surtout vers l'extérieur. Il a été pris en main et entièrement restauré par les antiquaires Jean-Philippe Demeyer, Frank Ver Elst et Jean-Paul Dewever, toujours en quête d'antiquités originales mais également actifs dans l'aménagement d'habitations dans un style éclectique. Ce style a d'ailleurs évolué au fil des ans vers un univers bariolé bondé d'objets excentriques et de beaucoup de couleurs. Ils ne reculent pas non plus devant quelques accents opulents voire kitsch qui donnent à leur intérieur un air de décor de théâtre. Ils ont créé plusieurs espaces de vie ou salons autour de la cour intérieure. Alors que l'orangerie privilégie la détente et le rustique, la pièce rez-de-jardin suggère plutôt la grande ville. La combinaison de vintage éclectique et des murs anciens a quelque chose de tonifiant. On pourrait dire qu'à leur façon, ils ont actualisé par des notes enjouées les recettes du célèbre décorateur anglais David Nightingale Hicks. Tout en étant parfaitement dans l'air du temps, leur style n'est pas aussi envahissant que beaucoup de créations soi-disant contemporaines. Et contrairement à de nombreux stylistes et architectes cramponnés à leur style et frileux par rapport aux tissus d'ameublement, nos antiquaires ne se retiennent pas dans leur envie de décoration.

ECLECTIC

These living rooms we find in a late medieval manor house not far from Bruges. The property lies next to the eighteenth-century Rooigem castle, but is much older than the castle itself. It is a typical Flemish brick building with a fairly robust architecture with few and relatively small windows. As such it feels somewhat closed off, at least to the outside. The house has been completely refurbished by antique dealers Jean-Philippe Demeyer, Frank Ver Elst and Jean-Paul Dewever, who as well as hunting down genuine antiquities and modernities also furnish homes in an eclectic style. Their style has evolved over the years into a bright environment full of eccentric objects and lots of colour. They are not afraid of rich or even here and there rather kitschy accents, which impart theatrical feel to their interiors. Around the courtyard they have created various seating and living spaces. The orangerie is rural and relaxing, while the conservatory has more of a city feel about it. The combination of eclectic vintage with old walls is refreshing. They have, in a way, updated the recipe of the celebrated English decorator David Nightingale Hicks with their own playful notes. Their style is modern, but not as in-your-eye as many so-called contemporary creations. Unlike many modern designers and architects who cling to their styles and are afraid of soft furnishing, these antique dealers go full steam ahead with decoration.

De combinatie van vintage met antiek en trouvailles zoals de palmboom, bovendien gepresenteerd in een landelijke context, is een hedendaagse mix. Deze kleurrijke zitkamer werd onlangs gerealiseerd in de voormalige oranjerie van het landgoed.

La combinaison de vintage avec des antiquités et quelques trouvailles comme ce palmier, de surcroît présentée dans un contexte rustique, correspond à un mélange très contemporain. Cet espace salon vient d'être aménagé récemment dans l'ancienne orangerie de la propriété.

The combination of vintage with antique and *trouvailles*, like the palm tree, presented moreover in a rural context, is very much a contemporary mix. This colourful lounge was recently put together in the former orangerie of the estate.

237

De middeleeuwse woonkamer met de geometrische wandschildering, geïnspireerd op een decor uit Damme. De bekleding van de stoelen is een hedendaagse interpretatie van het oude decor.

La salle de séjour médiévale avec la décoration murale géométrique, inspirée d'un décor à Damme. L'habillage des fauteuils est une interprétation contemporaine du décor ancien.

The medieval living room with the geometrical mural, inspired by a décor from Damme. The chair coverings are a contemporary interpretation of the historical décor.

FOLLY

DESIGN EN HAAIENTANDEN

Voor deze woning stappen we door het hart van Haarlem. We belanden er in het ongewone rariteitenkabinet van Bert Sliggers en Andrea de Wilde. Bert is als wetenschapper verbonden aan het beroemde Teylers Museum in Haarlem, een van de oudste musea van de Lage Landen, met schatten uit de kunst, de natuur en de wetenschappen. Het is dus een enorm kunst- en rariteitenkabinet. Het verwondert ons niet dat je daarvan de sporen in deze woning terugvindt. Bert Sliggers was al als kind een verwoed verzamelaar, die zowel bijzondere schelpen als haaien- en mensentanden verzamelde. Door zijn verzameling en de daaruit vloeiende nieuwsgierigheid werd hij geoloog, paleontoloog en mineraloog. Ook zijn vrouw Andrea deelt deze passie voor het ongewone. Ondertussen groeien hun verzamelingen doorheen het huis en verandert hun interieur om de haverklap. Nu zijn ze ook weg van vintage design. Hun rariteitenkabinet en bibliotheek maken een vast deel uit van het interieur. Daar zitten zelfs nog de trouvailles bij die Bert als kind verzamelde. Elke hoek heeft een andere sfeer, zoals de rood getinte Chinese inkomhal en het landelijk slaapvertrek met de borden van Fornasetti. Gezien Andrea ook in de mode actief is, houdt ze van wat hedendaagse accenten en kitsch. Beiden zijn tuk op grappige accenten en vinden designinterieurs te serieus.

DESIGN ET DENTS DE REQUIN

Dans le cœur de la ville de Haarlem, nous trouvons cette demeure qui abrite l'extraordinaire cabinet de curiosités de Bert Sliggers et Andrea de Wilde. Bert est chercheur au célèbre Musée Teylers à Haarlem, un des musées les plus anciens de tous les Pays-Bas et qui se consacre à l'art, la nature et les sciences. Il s'agit donc en fait d'un énorme cabinet d'art et de curiosités et il n'est guère étonnant qu'on en retrouve des traces dans cette maison. Tout gosse, Bert Sliggers était déjà un fervent collectionneur qui s'intéressait aussi bien à des coquillages particuliers qu'aux dents de requins et d'êtres humains. À travers cette collection et sa curiosité croissante, il est devenu géologue, paléontologue et minéralogiste. En plus, sa femme Andrea partage également cette passion de l'insolite. Aussi leurs collections ne cessent-elles de s'agrandir partout dans la maison et adaptent-ils à tout bout de champ leur intérieur. Outre leur collection, ils raffolent aussi du design vintage. Leur cabinet de curiosités et leur bibliothèque constituent des éléments permanents de leur intérieur. On y aperçoit même les trouvailles que Bert a faites dans son enfance. À chaque tournant, on découvre une ambiance différente, comme le vestibule chinois aux tonalités rouges ou la chambre à coucher champêtre avec les assiettes de Fornasetti. Comme Andrea s'active aussi dans le domaine de la mode, elle apprécie quelques touches contemporaines et kitsch. Tous deux adorent d'ailleurs mettre des accents comiques ne fût-ce que parce qu'ils trouvent les intérieurs design beaucoup trop sérieux.

DESIGN AND SHARK TEETH

For this home we step through the heart of Haarlem to end up in the unusual curiosities cabinet of Bert Sliggers and Andrea de Wilde. Bert works as a researcher at the famous Teyler Museum in Haarlem, one of the oldest museums in the Low Countries, full of treasures of art, nature and science. In short, an enormous art and curiosities cabinet. It comes as no surprise to find echoes of this in this apartment. As a child Bert Sliggers was an avid collector who gathered special shells, shark teeth and human teeth as well. Through his collection and the resulting sense of curiosity, he became a geologist, palaeontologist and mineralogist. His wife Andrea shares this passion for the unusual. Meanwhile their collections expand throughout the house, constantly changing the interior in the process. Right now they are mad on vintage design. Their curiosities cabinet and library are an integral part of the interior. In them you will still find the items Bert collected as a child. Each corner has a different atmosphere, like the red-tinted Chinese hall and the rural bedroom with the Fornasetti plates. Working as she does in fashion, Andrea is also keen to include some contemporary accents and kitsch. Both also like humorous accents and find design interiors too serious.

De bewoners van dit pand hebben een heel persoonlijke visie op wonen en verzamelen. Hun hart gaat naar heel uiteenlopende objecten met verhalen. In deze kast bijvoorbeeld, eigenlijk een deur van een Pakistaanse woning, liggen zelfs scherven en antieke tegels die tijdens de verbouwing van hun woning werden gevonden. Rechts bevinden we ons in de zithoek van de slaapkamer waar Piero Fornasetti even te gast is.

Les habitants de cette propriété ont développé une vision très personnelle sur la façon d'habiter et de collectionner. Ils se passionnent pour des objets très divers porteurs d'une histoire. Cette armoire, par exemple, qui est en réalité la porte d'une maison pakistanaise, contient même des débris de carreaux antiques trouvés lors de la rénovation de leur maison. À droite on pénètre dans le coin salon de la chambre à coucher où Piero Fornasetti s'est fait inviter.

This building's occupants have a highly personal vision of living and collecting. Their heart goes to very divergent objects, each with its own story to tell. In this dispay unit, for example, actually a doorway of a Pakistani house, are broken pieces of pottery and antique tiles they found during the renovation of their home. Right, we are in the sitting area of the bedroom where Piero Fornasetti is a guest.

VINTAGE & COUNTRY

COUNTRY

Lange tijd was de tegenstelling tussen 'modern' en 'klassiek' heel scherp. Moderne interieurs zouden steeds strak en ietwat koel zijn, klassieke interieurs warm en minder kaal. Dit contrast is uit den boze. In het begin van de eenentwintigste eeuw ontgroeiden beide tendensen het harnas waarin stijlen vroeger werden vastgesjord. Hoewel ook dat relatief is, want denk even aan decorateurs als David Hicks, die destijds moeiteloos jongleerde met stijlen. Hicks is trouwens weer in, wat erop wijst dat we weer mogen mengen. Interieurarchitect Catherine De Vil heeft de evolutie van de laatste jaren helemaal in haar vingers. In het begin van haar carrière werkte ze even voor de bekende decorateur Axel Vervoordt, maar ging daarna haar eigen weg. Haar liefde voor degelijke materialen en mooie proporties heeft ze wel bij Vervoordt op punt gesteld, en aanvankelijk was haar stijl ook landelijker. Dat merk je trouwens aan haar woning in de buurt van Lier. Vooral de woonkamer en eetkamer stralen nog die warme gloed van vroeger uit. Het gaat bovendien om een oud pand. Maar intussen heeft ze haar stijl geactualiseerd met wat uitgelezen design, fotografie en beeldende kunst. Haar interieur is helemaal van deze tijd, met oud en nieuw door elkaar, met enkele strakke, maar ook wat barokke elementen die voor een artistieke sfeer zorgen. Naast de woning staat haar atelier, dat eigenlijk een extra woonruimte is. Dit is haar living room voor de zomer, vol licht en met uitzicht op de tuin, het poolhouse en het zwembad.

COUNTRY

Pendant très longtemps, l'opposition entre 'moderne' et 'classique' a été très marquée. Les intérieurs modernes se devaient d'être rigides et quelque peu froids, les intérieurs classiques chaleureux et moins nus. Ce contraste a vécu. Au début du XXᵉ siècle, ces deux tendances se sont émancipées du corset dans lequel les différents styles se faisaient enserrer. Encore que... Il suffit de songer à des décorateurs comme David Hicks qui jonglaient sans efforts avec les styles. David Hicks revient d'ailleurs à la page, ce qui signifie qu'il ne faut pas avoir peur de mélanger les genres. L'architecte d'intérieur Catherine De Vil maîtrise parfaitement cette évolution des dernières années. Après avoir travaillé quelque temps au début de sa carrière pour le fameux décorateur Axel Vervoordt, elle a décidé de suivre sa propre voie. Certes, elle avait affiné chez Vervoordt sa prédilection pour les matériaux de qualité et les belles proportions et à l'origine, son style était tant soit peu plus rustique. Ce dont témoigne sa demeure dans les environs de Lier où surtout la salle à manger et le séjour respirent encore cette ambiance chaleureuse d'antan. Mais depuis, elle a actualisé son style par une sélection éclectique de design, de photographie et d'art plastique. Son intérieur a donc un air tout à fait contemporain, avec un mélange d'ancien et de moderne, avec quelques éléments très sobres et d'autres franchement baroques qui créent une ambiance artistique. Son atelier jouxtant la maison est en fait un espace de vie supplémentaire, c'est son séjour estival inondé de lumière, avec vue sur jardin, le pool house et la piscine.

COUNTRY

For a long time 'modern' and 'classical' were sharply opposed. Modern interiors were to be precise and on the cool side, classical interiors warm and less bare. This contrast is fundamentally wrong. In the first years of the 21st century both trends outgrew the straightjacket into which they had previously been lashed. Although even that, too, is relative: remember how designer David Hicks used to juggle effortlessly with styles. Hicks is once again in, telling us we're allowed to mix once again. Interior designer Catherine De Vil has the evolution of recent years in her fingers. She began her career with famous decorator Axel Vervoordt, but then went her own way. Her love of quality materials and fine proportions she refined with Vervoordt. Initially her style was also more rural. You see this in her house near Lier. The living and dining rooms especially radiate that warm glow of yesteryear. This is also an old property. But since then she has updated her style with exquisite design, photography and visual arts. Her interior is completely contemporary, with old and new together, with some tight-lined, but also rather baroque elements that give an artistic atmosphere. Next to the house is her studio that actually serves as an additional living space. This is her summer living room full of light and overlooking the garden, pool house and pool.

Interieurarchitecte Catherine De Vil interpreteert de landelijke stijl op een heel eigen manier. Haar stijl is artistiek en nonchalant. Hier stappen we door haar zomer-living room, ondergebracht in een gebouwtje in de tuin. Het is tevens haar werkplek. De combinatie van oude materialen werkt verfrissend. Bewonder even de Napolitaanse vloertegels die de moderne salontafel sieren. Op de volgende pagina wandelen we door het oude huis en door de eetkamer met antieke familieportretten.

L'architecte d'intérieur Catherine De Vil interprète le style rustique d'une manière toute personnelle. Son style est artistique et nonchalant. Voici son espace séjour estival, installé dans un petit bâtiment dans le jardin. C'est aussi son lieu de travail. La combinaison de matériaux anciens donne un air rafraîchissant : admirons, par exemple, ces carreaux napolitains qui recouvrent la table de salon moderne. La page suivante nous offre une visite dans la vieille maison avec la salle à manger décorée de vieux portraits de famille.

Interior architect Catherine De Vil interprets the country style in a very personal way. Her style is artistic and nonchalant. Here we step through her summer living room, housed in a small building in the garden. It is also her workplace. The combination of old materials is refreshing. We can also admire the Neapolitan tiles that decorate the modern coffee table. After this (next page) we walk through the old house, and the dining room with antique family portraits.

In het zomerhuis hangt een vakantiesfeer. En toch is dit ook de werkplek waar de inspiratie vandaan komt. Het is boeiend om te zien hoe Catherine met haar vintage meubilair omspringt, veel losser dan de meeste vintageverzamelaars, die niet zelden bang zijn voor een barok accent.

Dans la maison d'été, on respire un air de vacances et pourtant, c'est aussi le lieu de travail où Catherine puise son inspiration. Il est d'ailleurs passionnant de voir comment elle aborde son mobilier vintage, avec nettement plus de nonchalance que la plupart des collectionneurs de vintage souvent frileux devant la moindre touche baroque.

In the summer house a holiday atmosphere reigns. And yet this is also the workplace from where the inspiration comes. It is fascinating to see how Catherine handles her vintage furniture, much more flexibly than most vintage collectors who are often afraid of a baroque accent.

COSY

LANDELIJKE WONING

Dit is een gezellig interieur in Breda, waar je de charme van het verleden opsnuift en hier en daar toch een modern accent bespeurt. De bewoner, Emile van Dijk, houdt van warme, harmonieuze en schilderachtige interieurs. Deze interieurontwerper realiseert vooral in Nederland en België woningen en gaf verschillende inspirerende interieurboeken uit. Breda ligt bovendien bijna op de grens met België, op een steenworp van Antwerpen, en dat voel je zelfs in deze leefruimte. Hijzelf vindt Nederlandse interieurs doorgaans iets calvinistischer en strenger geordend, terwijl Vlaamse ietwat barokker zijn. Dat cliché klopt soms. Emile bewoont een oud pand in de mooie Catharinastraat, dat hij helemaal liet opknappen. Het heeft een neoklassiek voorhuis, een overdekte koer die nu deel uitmaakt van zijn living room en een achterhuis waar zijn zitkamer is gesitueerd. Vooral de middenruimte, een plek waar een nokvolle bibliotheek staat en waar Emile werkt, is fascinerend. Het is een verzamelkabinet met een artistieke uitstraling. Emile houdt van kunst aan de muur en verzamelt zowel modern als klassiek werk. Tussen de antieke meubels met een verschraalde patina zet hij wat design, bij wijze van verfrissende toets. Het geheel is op een aangename wijze nonchalant van stijl. Zijn stek heeft de charme van een landelijke woning in een kleine stad, en je komt er bovendien tot rust.

DEMEURE RUSTIQUE

Voici un intérieur convivial à Breda, où on baigne dans le charme du passé tout en détectant par-ci par-là des accents modernes. Son habitant, Emile van Dijk, affectionne les intérieurs chaleureux, harmonieux et picturaux. Réalisant surtout des intérieurs en Belgique et aux Pays-Bas, ce décorateur a également publié plusieurs livres dans le domaine de son métier. Et que Breda se situe quasiment sur la frontière belge à une encablure d'Anvers, se ressent jusque dans cet espace de vie. Il juge les intérieurs hollandais en général un peu plus calvinistes et plus strictement rangés que les intérieurs flamands qu'il trouve un tantinet plus baroques. S'il s'agit sans doute d'un cliché, il se voit néanmoins parfois confirmé. Emile habite une vieille maison dans la charmante Catharinastraat, qu'il a fait entièrement réhabiliter. Le devant néoclassique de la maison est suivi d'une cour couverte qui fait maintenant partie du séjour et d'une arrière-maison où il a installé le coin salon. Le plus fascinant est sans doute cet espace intermédiaire avec une bibliothèque surchargée qui est aussi son lieu de travail. On dirait un cabinet de collectionneur qui dégage un air artistique. Emile aime s'entourer d'art sur les murs et il collectionne aussi bien du moderne que du classique. Aux meubles anciens à la patine altérée, il ajoute une touche rafraîchissante en posant par-ci par-là du design. L'ensemble possède un style agréablement nonchalant. Bref, l'endroit qu'il s'est choisi a le charme d'une demeure rustique en plein milieu d'une petite ville où on retrouve en plus un calme apaisant.

AWAY-FROM-THE-CITY HOME

This is a cosy interior in Breda, where you sense the charm of the past and yet detect a modern accent here and there. Occupant Emile van Dijk likes warm, harmonious and picturesque interiors. This interior designer decorates homes mainly in the Netherlands and Belgium and has published several inspirational interior decoration books. Breda is also very close to the border with Belgium, a stone's throw from Antwerp. This you sense in this living room. Emile finds Dutch interiors generally somewhat more calvinistic and ordered, while Flemish ones are more baroque. That cliché is sometimes true. Emile lives in an old property in the attractive Catharinastraat, which he has totally refurbished. It has a neoclassical front part, a covered courtyard that is now part of his living room and a back part containing his sitting room. Particularly fascinating is the in-between area, with its bookcase crammed full of books, where Emile works – a collectors' cabinet with an artistic feel to it. Emile likes having art on his walls and collects both modern and classical works. Between the antique furnishings with their thin layer of patina he has placed some design objects to add a fresher note. The overall effect is pleasingly casual, with the charm of an away-from-the-city home in a small town offering genuine rest and relaxation.

Dit is een ongewone living room, want de tussenruimte die je ziet is een overdekte koer. Je herkent nog een buitenvenster en een buitendeur. De vele kunstwerkjes en objecten zorgen voor een schilderachtige harmonie. Emile van Dijk is de bewoner en decorateur die alles samenbracht, uiteraard in de loop der jaren. Dit is geen interieur dat in een handomdraai tot stand kwam, maar laat ons een leven van verzamelen zien. Een typische laat-twintigste-eeuwse collectie met wat antiek, wat vintage en moderne kunst.

Voici un séjour pour le moins insolite, car l'espace intermédiaire est en fait une cour couverte. On reconnaît d'ailleurs encore une porte et une fenêtre extérieures. Le grand nombre d'œuvres d'art et d'objets procure à l'ensemble une harmonie pittoresque. Le décorateur Emile van Dijk qui habite ici a pris de nombreuses années pour réunir tout ça. Cet intérieur n'a pas été aménagé en un clin d'œil, mais il témoigne d'une vie entière de collectionneur d'ailleurs très caractéristique pour la fin du XXᵉ siècle avec un peu d'antiquités, de vintage et d'art moderne.

This is an unusual living room, because the intermediate area you see is a covered courtyard. You can recognize an outside window and a door. The many works of art and *objets* produce a scenic harmony. Emile van Dijk is the occupant and decorator who brought it all together, of course over a number of years. This is not an interior that came about overnight, but the reflection of a life of collecting. A typical late 20th century collection with a mixture of antique, some vintage and modern art.

De tussenruimte, ooit een binnen-koertje, werd met oude plavuizen geplaveid, wat voor een antieke charme zorgt. Emile heeft de muren vervolgens behangen met prenten, tekeningen en schilderijen. Zijn stijl is naar Nederlandse normen vrij barok. Breda ligt nu eenmaal op een steenworp van Antwerpen.

Le sol de l'espace intermédiaire qui fut jadis une courette est recouvert d'anciennes dalles qui lui procurent un charme antique. Emile a choisi ensuite de décorer les murs d'une abondance d'images, de dessins et de tableaux. Pour des yeux néerlandais, son style est plutôt baroque, mais il est vrai que Breda n'est qu'à un jet de pierre d'Anvers.

The intermediate space, once a court-yard, is paved with ancient flagstones, which provide an antique charm. Emile has hung the walls with prints, drawings and paintings. His style is somewhat baroque by Dutch standards. Breda is just a stone's throw from Antwerp.

SAND HILL

WHITE BOX

Deze riante woning rust op een duin midden in het groen in Nieuwpoort, ongeveer op de grens tussen Frankrijk en België. Het gebouw heeft de vorm van een lange balk waarvan een van de lange zijden gericht is op de zon en uitzicht biedt op een wild duinenlandschap met knoestige bomen en doornstruiken. 'Aan de buitenkant heb ik de doos vrijwel gesloten', merkt architect Philippe Steyaert op, die hier samen met Sabine Van Praet – eveneens architect van vorming, maar actief in de fashionwereld – en hun vijf zonen woont. De voorgevel is een immens kamerscherm waarachter de woning zich opent naar het licht, dat extra wordt vastgehouden door de twee binnenterrassen. Hier is de grens tussen interieur en exterieur amper tastbaar. De grote leefruimte deelt zich op in een televisiehoek, een zitruimte en een eethoek, alle drie met een open haard. De woning biedt enkele bijzondere doorzichten, dwars door de leefruimte en door de gang met een vloer van grote, ietwat ruwe natuurstenen tegels. De combinatie van witte wanden met door de tand des tijds getaande vintagemeubels en een prachtige ruwe eettafel, net een kloostertafel, is perfect. En toch is het interieur allerminst strak of steriel. De ruwe vloeren en vele artistieke details zorgen voor een nonchalante sfeer. Philippe noch Sabine houden van wat ze 'de hedendaagse gladheid' noemen, van interieurs met een hoog laboratoriumgehalte. Veel hedendaagse villa's kijken uit op de natuur, zonder er echt mee in contact te treden. Hier leven ze met de natuur in huis, want van bij de eerste warmte staan alle vensters open. In dit huis is de gastvrijheid 'natuurlijk'.

WHITE BOX

Cette maison enchanteresse est posée sur une dune en pleine verdure à Nieuport, plus ou moins à cheval sur la frontière belgo-française. Avec sa forme de longue poutre dont un des longs côtés est orienté vers le soleil, elle regarde un paysage sauvage de dunes avec des arbres noueux et des roncières. « À l'extérieur, j'ai quasiment fermé la boîte », remarque l'architecte Philippe Steyaert qui occupe la maison avec Sabine Van Praet, également architecte de formation mais active dans l'univers de la mode, et leurs cinq fils. La façade principale est comme un immense paravent derrière lequel la maison s'ouvre à la lumière, retenue particulièrement pas les deux terrasses intérieures. Ici, la séparation entre intérieur et extérieur est à peine tangible. Le grand espace de vie se divise en coin télé, coin salon et coin salle à manger qui ont chacun une cheminée avec feu ouvert. La maison offre quelques belles percées qui traversent le séjour vers un couloir au sol revêtu de grandes dalles de pierre naturelle un peu rugueuse. Il y a aussi une combinaison parfaite des murs blancs avec des meubles vintage tannés par l'usure et une superbe table à manger brute qui a tout l'air d'une table de couvent. Mais en même temps, pas question de rigidité ni d'aspect stérile. Les sols bruts et les nombreux détails artistiques assurent l'ambiance de nonchalance. Ni Philippe ni Sabine n'apprécient ce qu'ils appellent le poli contemporain ou des intérieurs aux airs de laboratoire. Si beaucoup de villas contemporaines ont une vue sur la nature, très peu entrent véritablement en contact avec elle. Mais ici, on vit avec la nature dans la maison, car dès que la température le permet, toutes les fenêtres restent ouvertes. Dans cette maison, l'hospitalité est 'naturelle'.

WHITE BOX

This delightful house sits on a dune in the middle of a green area in Nieuwpoort, on the border between France and Belgium. The building has the shape of a long beam, with one of the long sides facing the sun and looking out over a landscape of wild dunes with gnarled trees and thorn-bushes. "On the outside I have pretty much closed the box", says architect Philippe Steyaert , who lives here with Sabine Van Praet – also an architect by training, but active in the fashion industry – and their five sons. The front façade is an immense screen behind which the house opens to the light that is also trapped by the two inner patios. Here the boundary between interior and exterior is barely tangible. The large living room divides into a TV corner, a lounge and a dining area, each with open fireplaces. The property offers some exceptional vistas, straight through the living room and down the hall with a floor of large, somewhat rough natural stone tiles. The combination of white walls with vintage furniture bronzed by the ravages of time and a beautiful rough wood dining table, just like a refectory table, is perfect. And yet the interior is anything but stiff or sterile. The rough floors and many artistic details provide a casual atmosphere. Neither Philippe nor Sabine love what they call contemporary smoothness, interiors with a high laboratory content. Many contemporary villas look out onto nature, without really coming into contact with it. Here they live with nature coming right into the house, because as soon as the weather warms up, all windows are open. In this house, hospitality is simply 'natural'.

Hier leef je met de natuur in huis. Eenmaal de ramen open, rollen de duinen gewoon binnen. Veel hedendaagse woningen staan wel in de natuur, maar hebben er amper een band mee. Hier is dat dus anders. Aan de zuidkant zijn er verschillende terrassen. Het interieur is vrij strak, maar alle objecten en meubels zijn wel precies gekozen.

Ici, on vit avec la nature dans la maison. Par beau temps, les dunes déboulent tout simplement par les fenêtres ouvertes. Si bon nombre de maisons contemporaines sont implantées dans la nature, rares sont celles qui ont un véritable lien avec elle. Avec les différentes terrasses côté sud, c'est vraiment différent ici. L'intérieur est plutôt sobre, mais tous les meubles et objets ont été choisis avec précision.

Here you live with nature right inside the house. Open the windows, and the dunes simply roll in. Many modern homes are built surrounded by nature, but with hardly any connection to it. Things are very different here. On the south side are several terraces. The interior is pretty pure-lined, but all objects and furniture are precisely chosen.

BRONZE

BRONZE

Niet alle kunstenaarswoningen zijn echt boeiend. Sommige zijn gewoon weinig meer dan een werkruimte zonder aankleding. Maar er zijn interieurs die ook het werk van de kunstenaar weerspiegelen. Daar is de woning van de Brusselse beeldhouwster Catherine François een mooi voorbeeld van. Het gaat om een oude villa uit het begin van de vorige eeuw met een grote woonruimte en tuin. De living heeft vele hoeken met kunstwerken, maar er staan ook enkele antieke meubels in uit familiebezit en een paar prachtige stukken vintagedesign. Maar het is geen cleane woonruimte met een uitgepuurd decor. Daar is Catherine François veel te spontaan voor. Ze begon op iets latere leeftijd beelden te maken. In het begin waren het vrij getourmenteerde creaties, die nu zoveel zachter en ronder zijn geworden. Haar werk is poëtisch geladen en esthetisch geraffineerd. Het sluit ook aan bij de grote beeldhouwtraditie uit de twintigste eeuw waarbij beeldhouwers zoals Henri Moore zich lieten inspireren door de natuurlijke vormen van keien en schelpen. Maar even terug naar de woonruimte, die artistiek en nonchalant is van stijl. Ook het coloriet van deze ruimte sluit aan bij haar werk. Je moet wel weten dat Catherine François heel veel tijd doorbrengt in haar studio, die achter in de tuin ligt. Haar atelier is een tweede woonruimte geworden.

BRONZE

Les demeures d'artistes ne sont pas toutes vraiment intéressantes. Certaines ne représentent guère plus qu'un espace de travail sans la moindre décoration. Mais il existe aussi des intérieurs qui reflètent l'œuvre d'un artiste et c'est certainement le cas de la maison habitée par la sculptrice bruxelloise Catherine François. Il s'agit d'une ancienne villa du début du siècle précédent avec un grand espace de vie et un jardin. Dans les nombreux coins du séjour sont placées des œuvres d'art mais aussi quelques meubles antiques de famille et quelques superbes pièces de design vintage. La spontanéité de Catherine François empêche cependant que le séjour présente un décor épuré ou trop 'clean'. En fait, elle s'est mise relativement tard à sculpter, réalisant d'abord des créations fort tourmentées pour évoluer ensuite vers des formes plus rondes et douces. D'un grand raffinement esthétique, son œuvre possède une grande puissance poétique. Elle se rallie aussi à la grande tradition sculpturale du xxe siècle dans laquelle des sculpteurs comme Henri Moore s'inspiraient des formes naturelles de cailloux et de coquillages. Mais pour revenir à l'espace de vie et son style artistique et nonchalant, on observe que les coloris aussi évoquent son œuvre. C'est vrai que Catherine François passe énormément de temps dans son studio au fond du jardin. Son atelier est devenu de fait un deuxième espace de vie.

BRONZE

Not all artists' homes are really fascinating. Some are little more than undecorated workspaces. But there are also interiors which reflect an artist's work. Like the home of Brussels sculptress Catherine François. This is an old detached house from the beginning of the last century, with a large living area and garden. The living room has lots of corners with artworks, together with some family antique furniture and a few beautiful pieces of vintage design. But it is not a hospital-clean living space with a purified décor. Catherine François is much too spontaneous for this. She started sculpting later in life. Her early pieces were rather tormented creations that have now become much softer and more rounded. Her work, poetically charged and aesthetically refined, falls within the broad sculptural tradition of the twentieth century, with sculptors like Henry Moore inspired by the natural shapes of pebbles and shells. But back to the living room, which is artistic and casual in style. The colouring of this space reflects that of her work. You need to know that Catherine François spends a lot of time in her studio in the back garden, which has become a second living room.

Je voelt dat dit de woning is van een kunstenaar en niet van een decorateur of architect. Dit is een spontaan en pretentieloos interieur vol leuke vondsten. Wat niet wegneemt dat wat er staat kwaliteit is. Kijk maar naar de zetel van hout en leder, een beeldhouwwerk. Ook de combinatie van wat kunst, vintage en een traditioneel burgerlijk maar mooi decor, werkt perfect.

On sent bien ici que c'est la maison d'une artiste et non d'un décorateur ou architecte. C'est un intérieur spontané et sans prétention plein de jolies trouvailles. Ce qui n'empêche pas que ce qui s'y trouve soit de bonne qualité comme en témoigne le siège en bois et cuir, une véritable sculpture. Par ailleurs, la combinaison d'un peu d'art et de vintage avec un décor bourgeois traditionnel mais très beau, est parfaitement réussie.

You feel that this is the home of an artist and not a decorator or architect. This is a spontaneous and unpretentious interior full of attractive finds. But even so everything bespeaks quality. Look at the wood and leather armchair, a sculpture in itself. Some artwork, vintage furniture and a traditional bourgeois, but pleasant, décor make a perfect combination.

CONTEM-
PORARY

CONTEMPORARY

Wie de eerste beelden van dit imposante landhuis ziet, wordt overweldigd door de monumentaliteit van dit project. Dat komt vooral door de asymmetrische dakconstructie, die het gebouw trouwens een hedendaags karakter schenkt. Toch is dat relatief, want het onregelmatige dak verwijst eigenlijk naar de oude boerderijen in de buurt. We bevinden ons in de schilderachtige Leiestreek nabij Gent, waar generaties kunstschilders het landschap op doek hebben vereeuwigd. Dat landschap is in deze woning alomtegenwoordig. Je krijgt het zelfs van onder de woning te zien, want onder de leefruimtes laat een vide het achterliggende weidelandschap bewonderen. Architect Eddy François voorzag de voorbouw trouwens van een rieten dak, om de traditie in huis te halen. Zonder oubolligheid, maar met een hedendaagse vormgeving. Het grote beschermende dak heeft wat van een tent waaronder tal van leefruimtes in elkaar klikken. De bruin-zwarte bakstenen geven het huis zowel binnen als buiten een stijlvolle stoerheid. François ontwerpt met de wabi-sabi-filosofie in het achterhoofd en houdt daarom van ruwe materialen en laat zijn gebouwen ook verouderen. Samen met zijn vrouw, interieurarchitecte Caroline De Wolf, runt hij de Gallery Beyond Argentaurum, waar zowel ontwerpers, beeldende kunstenaars als architecten welkom zijn. Via deze weg geraakte hij nauw bevriend met Andrea Branzi. Ook de kunst sluipt deze woning binnen. De Engelse kunstschilder Perry Roberts realiseerde hier een grote wandschildering die bijna van overal te zien is en de versmelting van kunst met architectuur versterkt.

CONTEMPORARY

Encountering this impressive country house for the first time, one is overwhelmed by its monumentality. This is produced primarily by the asymmetrical roof that gives the building a contemporary character. But in a relative way, as the irregular roof actually refers to the old farmhouses in the neighbourhood. We are in in the picturesque Leiestreek near Ghent, where generations of painters have immortalized the landscape on canvas. This landscape is omnipresent in this house. And indeed under the house, because through a vacant space under the living areas one can look out onto the meadow landscape behind. Architect Eddy François gave the front extension a thatched roof, in order to bring a sense of tradition, without being cheap or corny, into the contemporary design. The large protecting roof has about it something of a large tent, under which a series of living areas click together. The black-brown brick gives the house a stylish toughness both inside and outside. François designs with the wabi-sabi philosophy in mind, with a resulting love of raw materials, and also allows his buildings to age. Together with his wife, interior designer Caroline De Wolf, he runs the Gallery Beyond Argentaurum, where designers, artists and architects are all welcome. In this way he became close friends with Andrea Branzi. Art also sneaks inside this house. English painter Perry Roberts did here a large mural that can be seen from almost everywhere and which strengthens the fusion of art and architecture.

CONTEMPORAIN OF CONTEMPORARY

Les premières images de ce manoir impressionnant en imposent instantanément par le caractère monumental du projet qui provient notamment de la toiture asymétrique. Celle-ci confère indiscutablement une touche contemporaine à l'habitation et pourtant, elle rappelle en fait les anciennes fermes de la région. On se trouve en effet dans ce paysage pittoresque de la Lys près de Gand que des générations de peintres ont immortalisé sur la toile. Un paysage d'ailleurs omniprésent dans cette demeure puisqu'on peut même admirer les prés derrière la maison à partir d'un vide aménagé sous les espaces de vie. Soucieux d'amener un peu de tradition dans la maison sans faire ringard, l'architecte Eddy François a pourvu l'avant-corps d'un toit en chaume d'un modèle contemporain. Le grand toit abritant la maison a un petit air de tente sous laquelle s'emboîtent un grand nombre d'espaces de vie. Les briques d'un brun très sombre confèrent une impression de robustesse stylée. Comme le travail de création de François s'inspire de la philosophie wabi-sabi, il affectionne les matériaux bruts et laisse aussi vieillir ses constructions. Avec son épouse, l'architecte d'intérieur Caroline De Wolf, il tient la Gallery Beyond Argentaurum où ils accueillent aussi bien des stylistes que des artistes plasticiens et des architectes. C'est par ce biais qu'il s'est lié d'amitié avec Andrea Branzi. L'art n'est d'ailleurs pas passé sans s'arrêter dans cette maison : l'artiste peintre anglais Perry Roberts y a réalisé une grande fresque visible de presque partout et qui renforce la fusion entre l'art et l'architecture.

Terwijl je deze woning doorstapt, flitsen je allerlei beelden door het hoofd. Je denkt ontegensprekelijk aan Carlo Scarpa, de beroemde Italiaanse architect die virtuoos omsprong met beton en doorzichten. Dat doet architect Eddy François ook meesterlijk. Hij reist trouwens veel door Italië. Hier zien we de centrale leefruimte met de prachtige haard, het balkon van een klein bureau en een doorzicht naar het landschap.

En traversant cette demeure, on est submergé d'images qui jaillissent à l'esprit. Ainsi songe-t-on irrémédiablement au célèbre architecte italien Carlo Scarpa, le virtuose du béton et des perspectives. C'est ce que réussit aussi magistralement l'architecte Eddy François, qui voyage d'ailleurs souvent en Italie. Voici l'espace de vie central avec la superbe cheminée, le balcon d'un petit bureau et une vue sur le paysage.

As you step through this house all kinds of images flash through your head. You cannot but think of Carlo Scarpa, the famous Italian architect with his virtuoso handling of concrete and vistas. Eddy François is also a master in this. He travels a lot around Italy. Here we see the central living room with its superb fireplace, the balcony of a small office corner and the view out onto the landscape.